ON THE ORIGIN OF SPECIES:
YOUNG READERS EDITION

For Gretchen Newberry,
scientist and friend
—R.S.

𝒜
atheneum

ATHENEUM BOOKS FOR YOUNG READERS
An imprint of Simon & Schuster Children's Publishing Division
1230 Avenue of the Americas, New York, New York 10020
Young Readers adaptation of Charles Darwin's *On the Origin of Species* copyright © 2018 by Rebecca Stefoff
Jacket and interior illustrations (excluding illustrations credited herein to other parties) copyright © 2018 by Teagan White
Page 168 constitutes an extension of the copyright page.
For information about special discounts for bulk purchases, please contact Simon & Schuster Special Sales
at 1-866-506-1949 or business@simonandschuster.com.
The Simon & Schuster Speakers Bureau can bring authors to your live event. For more information or to book an event,
contact the Simon & Schuster Speakers Bureau at 1-866-248-3049 or visit our website at www.simonspeakers.com.
Jacket design by Sonia Chaghatzbanian; interior design by Irene Metaxatos
The text for this book was set in Adobe Caslon Pro.
Teagan White's illustrations for this book were rendered in graphite and watercolor with digital coloring.
Manufactured in China
0718 SCP
First Edition
2 4 6 8 10 9 7 5 3 1
Library of Congress Cataloging-in-Publication Data
Names: Stefoff, Rebecca, 1951– author. | White, Teagan, illustrator. | adaptation of (work): Darwin, Charles, 1809–1882. On the origin of species.
Title: Charles Darwin's On the origin of species / adapted by Rebecca Stefoff ; with illustrations by Teagan White.
Other titles: On the origin of species
Description: Young readers edition. | First edition. | New York : Atheneum, [2018]
Identifiers: LCCN 2017042047 | ISBN 9781481462495 (hardcover) | ISBN 9781481462518 (eBook)
Subjects: LCSH: Evolution (Biology)—Juvenile literature. | Natural selection—Juvenile literature.
Classification: LCC QH367.1 .S74 2018 (print) | DDC 576.8/2—dc23
LC record available at https://lccn.loc.gov/2017042047

Charles Darwin's

ON THE ORIGIN OF SPECIES

YOUNG READERS EDITION

Adapted by **Rebecca Stefoff**

with illustrations by **Teagan White**

ATHENEUM BOOKS FOR YOUNG READERS

New York London Toronto Sydney New Delhi

CONTENTS

Darwin's Great Discovery

Poor man, he just stands and stares at a yellow flower for minutes at a time," said the gardener. "He would be far better off with something to do."

The gardener was talking about his employer, an English gentleman named Charles Darwin. What the gardener didn't realize was that while Darwin spent a lot of time looking at nature, he *was* doing something. He was planning a revolution in science.

The revolution began in 1859, when Darwin published *On the Origin of Species*. The book sold out in a few days. It caused an uproar in the scientific community and beyond. Eventually it changed our understanding of all living things.

In 2015 a panel of British booksellers, librarians, publishers, and scholars listed twenty of the most important academic or scholarly books ever written. They asked the public to choose the one that had had the biggest influence on the world. The public voted for Darwin's *Origin*.

A portrait of Charles Darwin, painted
in the late 1830s.

Beetles, the *Beagle*, and Barnacles

Charles Darwin was born in 1809 in Shrewsbury, England. As a boy, he was not an outstanding student—a fact that once caused his exasperated father to tell young Charles that he would be "a disgrace to yourself and all your family." Darwin was sent to medical school in Scotland so that he could become a doctor like his father, but he lacked interest in his studies. He was also sickened by surgical operations, which were performed on terrified, screaming patients before the development of anesthetics to make them unconscious. In 1828 he switched to studying to become a clergyman at Christ's College, Cambridge.

Darwin was already deeply interested in natural history. That broad term covers the study of the natural world: rocks, fossils, weather, geography, and all the biological sciences. In Darwin's day, people who studied natural history were

H.M.S. BEAGLE IN STRAITS OF MAGELLAN. MT. SARMIENTO IN THE DISTANCE. *Frontispiece.*

This drawing of the *Beagle* in the Strait of Magellan, near the southern tip of South America, was published in 1890, long after the voyage. It is based on an earlier drawing by one of Darwin's shipmates.

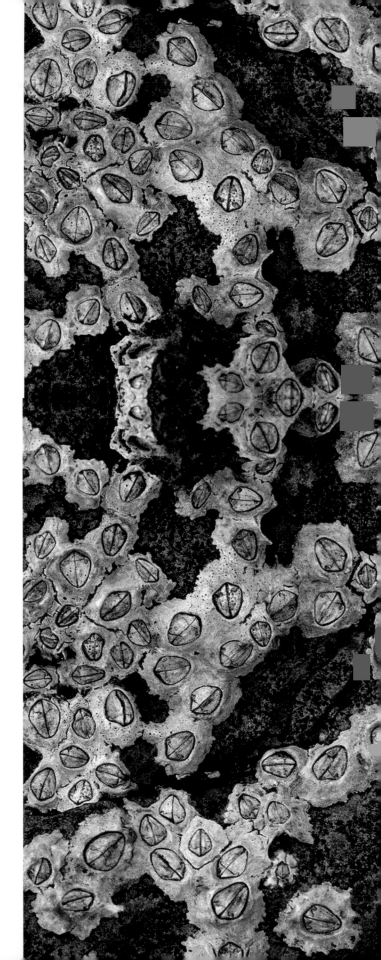

known as naturalists. Some were professors or lecturers at schools, or worked for museums. Many held other positions and pursued natural history in addition to their work. A clergyman—as Darwin was expected to become after leaving medical school—could also be a naturalist.

Geology and biology were Darwin's main passions. He became an enthusiastic collector of beetles. One of his specimens turned out to be a new species, and Darwin received credit in a scientific journal for discovering it.

At college, Darwin found a group of fellow students and professors who were also passionately interested in natural history. He began to be known as a promising naturalist. After completing his studies in 1831, he was invited to join a naval ship called the HMS *Beagle* on a long voyage around the world. His role aboard ship was unofficial, a combination of naturalist and companion to the captain. The voyage lasted for almost five years. Much of the time was spent along the coasts of South America, but the *Beagle* also visited Tahiti, New Zealand, and South Africa. Darwin took every opportunity to explore and to gather insects, plants, and animals from environments such as rain forests, deserts, grasslands, and coral reefs.

The *Beagle* spent a month in the Galápagos Islands, west of South America. There, Darwin marveled at—and collected samples of—the variety of lifeforms scattered across the small volcanic isles. Darwin's groundbreaking later work would draw on everything he observed during the *Beagle*'s voyage, including important bird specimens he collected in the Galápagos.

Darwin never did any more serious traveling, and he never became a clergyman. Family money and wise investments meant that he did not have to work for a living. After the *Beagle* voyage, he plunged into the life of a full-time naturalist. He had made a name for himself during the trip with letters to other naturalists. Once back in England, he wrote a book about the *Beagle*'s voyage. He also edited five volumes about the zoology of the voyage and wrote three volumes about its geology.

During this time Darwin married his cousin Emma Wedgwood. They started a family and moved to a country estate called Down House, where Darwin would live for the rest of his life. There, Darwin spent the years 1846 to 1854 in an intense research project. His goals were to sharpen his knowledge of biology and to gain credit as a serious scientist.

A biologist was expected to be an expert on some particular group of species. Darwin chose barnacles: relatives of crabs and lobsters that attach themselves to rocks, ships, and other animals. For years, parts of his home were filled with these shelly specimens. His children grew so used to this that one of them asked a friend, "Where does your father keep his barnacles?" Between 1851 and 1854 Darwin published four volumes about living and fossil barnacles. They were at once recognized as the world's leading works on the subject. Barnacle researchers today still rely on them.

But even before he married and began the barnacle project, Darwin had been quietly working on another idea, one that he had started thinking about during the *Beagle* voyage. This idea would make Darwin one of the most famous and controversial naturalists in history. He called it "the species question."

The Big Idea

Darwin's big idea was about how species change over long periods of time. He was not the first naturalist to explore this idea. A few in his time and even earlier had pondered what they called "the transmutation of species" ("transmutation" means "change in form"). In fact, Darwin's grandfather Erasmus Darwin had published several works touching on the subject.

The idea that species might be mutable, or capable of permanent change, was extremely difficult to accept for most people of Darwin's day, including many scientists. The traditional view was that each species had been divinely created in its present form. Some naturalists did argue that species changed over time, but even those who defended the transmutation of species could

> **A species is a group of organisms in which all individuals could interbreed to produce fertile offspring. Chapter One has more details on Darwin's definition of "species" and how scientists use the word today.**

not give a convincing explanation of *how* species might change.

Darwin would offer that explanation.

His early work on "the species question" is recorded in a notebook he started in 1837. During the *Beagle* voyage he had been "much struck" by how various species of plants and animals were spread across South America. He had also noticed fossils that pointed to a link between the living and extinct species of that continent. "These facts," he wrote much later, "seemed to me to throw some light on the origin of species." Darwin began gathering more facts that might help him solve the mystery of how species come into being.

By the end of 1838 he had worked out his theory. He wrote a summary of it in 1842. Two years later he prepared a longer version. That's when he first shared some thoughts on the subject, in a letter to a friend and fellow naturalist, the botanist Joseph Hooker. Darwin wrote that "gleams of light have come, & I am almost convinced . . . that species are not (it is like confessing a murder) immutable [unchanging]." He added, "I think I have found out . . . the simple way by which species become exquisitely adapted. . . ."

Darwin made the point that living things can and often do change from generation to generation. The changes may be small, but over time, as they are passed from parents to descendants, they build up into greater and greater differences, until new species are formed. Darwin called this pattern "descent with modification." Another term for it is "evolution."

The heart of Darwin's theory was his explanation of *how* such changes could occur. They came about, Darwin reasoned, though a process that he called "natural selection." He would spend twenty years gathering information to support this idea, which would eventually reach the world in *On the Origin of Species*.

A notebook from 1837–1838 contains Darwin's first attempt to sketch a "tree of life."

What Darwin Knew and Didn't Know

Darwin broke new ground on "the species question," but his work was still shaped by the state of scientific knowledge of his time. Darwin was helped by new scientific advances, but he was held back by gaps in what was known.

When Darwin began his work, most scientists and many other people had accepted the idea of "deep time," or geological time, as it is now usually called. This concept started with an eighteenth-century Scottish geologist named James Hutton. He claimed that the physical history of the Earth, which could be read from its geology, had unfolded over long, long ages—much longer than previously thought.

Geological time was further developed by Charles Lyell, a leading British geologist. Lyell put the age of the Earth at more than three hundred million years, a figure that Darwin echoed in the *Origin*. This deep past was essential to Darwin's theory, which argued that evolution by natural selection took place over long periods of time. Neither Lyell nor Darwin, however, grasped the true depth of geological time. Scientists today place the age of the Earth at about 4.54 billion years.

Long before Darwin, people wondered about the strange stony forms they occasionally dug out of the ground. Some, such as stone seashells found on mountaintops far from the sea, were especially puzzling. Others resembled no known living creatures. By Darwin's time, most naturalists understood that these odd objects were fossils, remains of animals and plants that had once been alive.

Starting in the 1820s, fossils of dinosaurs opened a window on a distant

300,000,000

This Book

This version of Darwin's *On the Origin of Species* is based on the first edition of the book, published in 1859. It has been adapted, or changed, in several ways.

First, Darwin's text has been shortened. The original *Origin* is more than three times as long as the chapters that follow. Some sections have been omitted because they are out of date. In Chapter Five, for example, Darwin covered the topic of heredity. His main idea was sound, but parts of the chapter are now known to be inaccurate, so they have been cut.

In addition, throughout the *Origin*, Darwin piled up mountains of evidence to support his theory, because he knew that people would find it hard to accept. To save space, this version often reduces half a dozen examples to just one or two. And in all chapters, material has been dropped or shortened for easier reading. For example, Chapter Eleven is a shorter version of material that Darwin spread over two long chapters. The goal of these changes was to preserve the building blocks of Darwin's thought, while streamlining his presentation.

Second, Darwin's language has been simplified in many places. Long sentences and paragraphs have been broken up into shorter ones. Some unfamiliar terms have been replaced with familiar ones. (There is also a glossary of terms in the back of this book.) Still, the goal was to preserve as much of Darwin's original language as possible—especially the many passages that have become famous for their beauty and enthusiasm.

Third, some chapter titles and headings are new, and occasional brief notes have been added next to the text, to define terms and guide readers through the book. You will also find short articles in boxes like this one. These notes and short articles do not come from the *Origin*; they have been written especially for this adaptation. Like the photographs and illustrations chosen for this book, these articles help bring the science up to date from Darwin's day, fill in the blanks that he did not know, and show some of the ways in which the study of evolution itself has evolved since his time.

ON

THE ORIGIN OF SPECIES

BY MEANS OF NATURAL SELECTION,

OR THE

PRESERVATION OF FAVOURED RACES IN THE STRUGGLE
FOR LIFE.

By CHARLES DARWIN, M.A.,

FELLOW OF THE ROYAL, GEOLOGICAL, LINNÆAN, ETC., SOCIETIES;
AUTHOR OF 'JOURNAL OF RESEARCHES DURING H. M. S. BEAGLE'S VOYAGE
ROUND THE WORLD.'

LONDON:
JOHN MURRAY, ALBEMARLE STREET.
1859.

The right of Translation is reserved.

past that teemed with life-forms very different from those of the present. Most naturalists agreed that the strange life-forms had become extinct, although they could not explain why. The knowledge that species *could* become extinct, to be known only by their fossil remains, became part of Darwin's theory, which said that new species develop from earlier ones and then replace them. Scientists did not yet know, however, that the ancient Earth had seen episodes of mass extinction that wiped out large percentages of all existing species in fairly short periods of geological time.

Another important thing Darwin didn't know was how traits pass from parents to their offspring. He admitted in the *Origin* that the mechanism of heredity was a mystery. It was plain to see, however, that traits *do* get passed from one generation to the next, and this fact is one of the foundations of Darwin's theory. His work was only strengthened by later discoveries about the mechanisms of heredity—DNA, genes, and chromosomes.

Darwin's theory was about how life changes its forms over time. He said nothing about how life itself came into existence. That is a question that scientists today are still working to answer.

Darwin's Difficulties

Why did claiming that species were capable of permanent change feel like "confessing a murder" to Darwin? Why did he wait so long to publish his theory?

One reason is that the public and many scientists had reacted with hostility to an 1844 book called *Vestiges of the Natural History of Creation*. Its author, Robert Chambers, had said that species must have evolved through some kind of natural process and were not the result of divine creation. Darwin was a gentle and shy person. He did not look forward to the storm of criticism or even outrage that he felt sure his own work would unleash.

Another reason is that Darwin wanted to make sure his theory was supported by a wealth of evidence. He spent years building up that evidence and testing every part of his theory to make sure he had answers for questions or criticisms. During this time, the patient work on barnacles strengthened not only his scientific reputation but also the case for his theory.

Darwin also suffered from repeated bouts of sickness and long periods when he was exhausted and could barely work. The deaths of his father in 1848 and his beloved daughter Annie in 1851 brought lasting grief and slowed his progress. But finally, in 1856, at the urging of botanist Joseph Hooker and geologist Charles Lyell, Darwin began writing what he called the "everlasting species-Book."

Naturalist Alfred Russel Wallace, shown here in 1895, came up with the same theory as Darwin about the origin of species.

In addition to criticism, Darwin's ideas drew ridicule, such as this 1871 cartoon published in *Hornet* magazine. Darwin wrote to a friend, "I keep all these things. Have you seen me in the *Hornet*?"

Two years later, Darwin had written more than half of the book when he had a terrible shock. A British naturalist named Alfred Russel Wallace wrote to Darwin from an island in what is now the Asian nation of Indonesia. Wallace wanted Darwin's opinion of a paper he had written on how new species come into existence. When Darwin read the paper, he realized that Wallace had come up with a theory almost identical to the theory of natural selection that Darwin had been working on for so long.

Darwin wanted to be fair to Wallace, but he knew that he had been first with the idea. He turned to Lyell for advice. Together with Hooker, Lyell arranged for part of Darwin's 1844 summary of his theory and Wallace's paper to be read aloud together at a scientific meeting. Both men received credit for the discovery, but it was clear that Darwin had made it first.

The *Origin* Then and Now

Once his theory was out in the open, Darwin hurriedly completed a shorter-than-planned version of his book, which was published as *On the Origin of Species*. As he had feared, its appearance in 1859 caused a sensation. Some scientists supported Darwin's theory; others rejected it. Many religious believers and clergy were appalled by the vision of life governed by natural rather than divine law. Some leading ministers, however, publicly supported Darwin and pointed out that evolution did not banish God. The American preacher Henry Ward Beecher wrote, "I regard evolution as being the discovery of the Divine method in creation."

Controversy over the *Origin* had not disappeared by the time Darwin died in 1882, but by then Darwin's views on evolution were accepted by many scientists. It took longer for natural selection to be accepted as the mechanism of evolution, but evidence for it continued to mount. Today, evolution by natural selection is recognized as one of the foundations of our knowledge of biology.

Darwin called the *Origin* "one long argument" for the theory that species are not created individually but are descended from other species. The entire book is a carefully built model of scientific thinking. It shows a scientist striving to answer a question. The scientist first collects research that might help answer the question, then comes up with a hypothesis—an answer that seems to explain the facts. The next step is testing the hypothesis, either by performing experiments or by seeking out evidence for or against the hypothesis. (Darwin did both.) Finally, the scientist analyzes the results to see if they support the hypothesis.

The question Darwin wanted to answer was, "How do species come into being?" The *Origin* lays out the steps of his answer. It starts with the well-known fact that breeders of domestic plants and animals can create new **varieties**, with new features and habits. This fact would have been part of everyday life for many readers in Darwin's time, when large numbers of people were familiar with raising plants and livestock. The changes brought about by plant and animal breed-

Varieties are different forms within the same species. The following chapters will show how Darwin used this term and the related term "subspecies."

ers are the first step in Darwin's argument. He then goes on to say that the same thing has been happening, on a much larger and longer scale, throughout nature for as long as life has existed.

Darwin's grand theory blossoms from Chapter One, a close look at things as ordinary as pigeons and roses.

—R.S.

Sporting Plants and Blue Pigeons

When we look at plants and animals that have been **domesticated** for a long time, we see many differences among members of the same species. Individual plants or animals of these species show more differences from one another than those of a wild species show. Domesticated species also exist in more varieties. Think, for example, of the many different kinds of domesticated pigeon, dog, corn, or rosebush.

Domesticated species have produced variations since people began tending plants and taming animals. This is because we raise these species under a wide variety of conditions, often different from their natural conditions. It seems clear, however, that organisms must live for several generations

Domesticated plants and animals belong to species that have been tamed or cultivated and bred by humans. They are farmed, tended, herded, or raised rather than living in a wild or natural state.

Wheat still produces new variations, even though it has been domesticated for ten thousand years or so.

Darwin used "variation" to mean a difference from the standard or norm for the species. Scientists in Darwin's time did not understand how or why variations occur in plants and animals. Darwin will return to this mystery later in this chapter and in several of the chapters ahead. See "The Missing Piece" in Chapter Five for the modern scientific explanation.

Heritable "characters" (Darwin's word for "features") pass from parents to offspring—in other words, these features are inherited by offspring from their parents.

The structure of a plant or animal is its inner and outer form—how it looks as well as how it is put together inside.

under new conditions before they begin to show much variation.

Once variation has begun, new traits generally keep appearing for many generations. Our oldest cultivated plants, such as wheat, still often yield new varieties. Our oldest domesticated animals, such as goats and sheep, can still produce new varieties. I suspect that most **variations happen** when the reproductive elements of parents are changed in some way, causing changes to appear in their offspring.

New and Very Different Plants

Gardeners speak of "sporting plants." They mean a single bud or branch that suddenly takes on a new appearance, very different from the rest of the plant. Gardeners can then cause these "sports" to spread or reproduce by breeding new plants from them. Sporting plants are extremely rare in nature, but very common in plants that are cultivated by humans.

Sporting plants are one kind of variation. Another kind of variation appears in the offspring of plants and animals. Seedling plants grown from the same fruit sometimes differ considerably from one another. So do young animals from the same litter. This happens even when the young plants or animals had the same conditions of life as their parents.

Changes in one feature often go along with changes in other, unrelated features. Cats with blue eyes, for example, are likely to be deaf. White sheep and pigs may react differently to certain vegetable poisons than colored animals do. Pigeons with feathered feet have skin between their outer toes, unlike other pigeons. In another example, pigeons with short beaks have small feet, and pigeons with long beaks have large feet. If breeders of domesticated plants or animals go on breeding individuals to strengthen any one feature, they will almost certainly bring about other changes as well.

Heritable characters may have to do with an organism's physical appearance, or its internal **structure**, or the way it behaves. There is an endless number of these variations. Some are trivial. Some are important. But no breeder doubts that some of these variations pass from parents to offspring. The breeder's basic belief is "like produces like," meaning that parents produce offspring who resemble them.

Everyone must have heard of cases of albinism or hairy bodies that appear in several members of the same family, which means that they are heritable. If these strange and rare characters can be inherited, more ordinary and common variations must be inherited too.

The Unknown Laws

Mysterious laws govern the way variations occur within a species. We see only a few of these laws, and dimly. But **other laws**, those that govern how offspring inherit characters, are completely unknown.

No one can say why the same peculiar character is sometimes inherited and sometimes not. Why does a child sometimes look much like its grandfather or grandmother, or an even more remote ancestor? Why do parents pass certain features to their children of both sexes, while other features pass only to sons or to daughters?

The same uncertainty appears when we try to draw a line between a variety and a subspecies, or between a subspecies and a species. Almost all domestic animals and plants have been called mere varieties by some experts but distinct species by other experts.

When we try to estimate how much the varieties of a domesticated species differ from one another, we are soon in doubt. We do not know whether our domesticated varieties descended from one parent species, or several. If this point could be cleared up, the results would be interesting. If, for instance, it could be shown that the greyhound, bloodhound, terrier, spaniel, and bulldog are all varieties of a single species, that would show how much a

Darwin returns to the question of these "other laws" in Chapter Five.

A "sporting branch," different in size and structure from the rest of the tree, springs from a dwarf Alberta spruce.

species may vary. And if one species could produce so many varieties, we might begin to doubt that species that are very closely related—such as the many species of foxes that live in different parts of the world—could never have changed.

In the case of most animals and plants that were domesticated in ancient times, I do not think we can know for sure whether they have descended from one or several species. The whole subject must, I think, remain vague. With respect to **horses**, I am inclined to believe that all the varieties have descended

Darwin was right about horses. Existing horses are surviving subspecies of a single extinct species.

Darwin and other scientists were curious about the origins of domesticated animals, such as the cattle of ancient Egypt. This model stable was made around 1975 BCE, during Egypt's Middle Kingdom.

What Is a Species?

Scientists today generally define a species as any group of organisms that could all interbreed and produce fertile offspring. This means that the offspring could *also* produce offspring.

For example, lions and tigers both belong to the genus *Panthera*, but they are different species. Lions and tigers do not typically mate with one another in the wild. In zoos they sometimes mate and even produce young, but those young are sterile—they cannot reproduce. To be considered the same species, two organisms must produce offspring that can reproduce.

Many species are divided into smaller groups called "subspecies." A subspecies is a group of plants or animals that are recognizably different from the standard appearance or structure of their species, but not different enough to be considered a separate species. Modern scientists also sometimes use the term "variety" to refer to a subgroup that has not been officially recognized as a subspecies. Unlike different species, varieties and subspecies within the same species can usually interbreed. They generally *don't* interbreed, however, because they live in different places or have different habits and seldom come into contact.

In Darwin's day, naturalists could not agree on how much difference they had to see between two groups of plants or animals in order to call them separate species. Darwin used the terms "species," "subspecies," and "variety" throughout the *Origin*, but not always as scientists define them today.

For Darwin, "species" was a loose, somewhat flexible category. It was broader and more inclusive than "subspecies" or "variety," but narrower than "genus." He viewed a species as a group of organisms that were descended from the same ancestor and that shared some distinctive feature of form, structure, or behavior. To Darwin, varieties within a species were steps on the way to subspecies, and subspecies were steps on the way to separate species. But as you will see in Chapter Eight, where Darwin writes about interbreeding, he thought that the barrier between species sometimes had gaps—more like a fence than a solid wall.

Two ligers—offspring of a male lion and a female tiger—in a zoo.

from one wild stock. Some authors, however, have carried to an absurd extreme the idea that domesticated varieties of animals and plants have come from more than one wild species. One author believes that Great Britain used to have eleven wild species of sheep found nowhere else, and that each species was the source of a modern breed!

The explanation, I think, is simple. Naturalists who spend a long time studying varieties are strongly impressed with the differences between them. They

The Making of the Modern Dog

Suppose you had never seen a dog. Then one day you saw a Great Dane next to a Chihuahua—one creature large, with floppy ears and a big jaw, the other tiny, with upstanding ears and a pointed jaw. Would you think they belonged to the same species? Or to different species, maybe related ones, like a tiger and a lion?

All dogs belong to the same species, even though they come in a vast variety of shapes and sizes. Dogs that have certain well-marked features, such as the Chihuahua's small size and large eyes, are said to belong to "breeds." As of March 2018, 190 breeds were recognized by the American Kennel Club, which runs dog shows and keeps records of dog breeding in the United States. More than a hundred other breeds are recognized by other organizations around the world. Many dogs, however, combine the features of more than one breed. These dogs may be called "mutts" or "mongrels."

Where dogs came from remains something of a mystery. Darwin thought that dogs were probably domesticated from several wild species. By the 1990s, scientists decided that Darwin was wrong. All domesticated dogs, they said, descended from *Canis lupus*, the gray wolf. The only question was whether dogs should be called *Canis lupus familiaris*, a subspecies of gray wolf, or *Canis familiaris*, a separate species.

In 2013 some researchers put forward a new idea. Based on a study of DNA from dogs and wolves around the world, they claimed that dogs descended from a type of wolf that is now extinct. More research is under way, but experts do not yet agree on where, when, and how dogs evolved from wolves.

Most breeds of modern dog, however, have been created during the past few centuries. The many breeds we see today came about because people decided what features they wanted in dogs, and then bred males and females with those features in order to produce pups with a high chance of having the desired features.

Like all species, dogs occasionally vary in some of their features, due to random genetic mutation. This fact allowed breeds to be created. For example, a dog might have been born with unusually fluffy hair or longer legs or a gentler temper than most other dogs. That dog might pass those features to its offspring. If it mated with a dog that also had those features, the offspring could be even more likely to inherit them.

If people liked dogs with fluffy hair or long legs or gentle tempers, they would notice and take care of dogs with those features. By deliberately breeding them and their offspring, people would

A labradoodle, one of the new dog types created recently through artificial selection.

cause the chosen features to appear ever more strongly in a subgroup of dogs. Over thousands or just hundreds of years, that subgroup could become a distinctive breed—although members of that breed could still produce offspring with any other dog.

Darwin used the term "artificial selection" for the way humans control the breeding of plants and animals to create varieties they want. He understood that it is in some ways like a sped-up version of what happens in nature. Unlike nature, though, humans create breeds and varieties tailored specially to their own needs and desires. They're still doing it. Breeders today have created new kinds of dogs such as the labradoodle (a hybrid of Labrador retriever and poodle) and the puggle (a hybrid of pug and beagle).

No dog breed has yet become its own species, but the making of the modern dog shows just how much a species can change in a short time.

Great Dane (*left*) and Chihuahua (*right*).

refuse to see that large differences may be the result of small differences that have built up over many generations. Yet many naturalists know far less about heredity than breeders know. Should they not be cautious when they mock the idea that species are descended from other species?

The Case of the Pigeon

Believing that it is always best to study some special group, I have taken up domesticated pigeons. I have kept every breed I could get, and I have been most kindly given skins from several quarters of the world. These birds illustrate the great variety produced by artificial selection.

The diversity of breeds is astonishing. The English carrier pigeon, especially the male bird, is remarkable for the fleshy naked skin about its head. This is accompanied by long eyelids, very large nostrils, and a wide mouth. The beak of the short-faced tumbler pigeon has an outline almost like that of a finch. The common tumbler flies at a great height in a compact flock, and tumbles in the air head over heels. The runt is a pigeon of great size, with a long, massive beak and large feet. The trumpeter and laugher utter a very different coo from the other breeds. The fantail has thirty or even forty tail feathers, instead of the normal twelve or fourteen.

Great as the differences are between the breeds of domesticated pigeons, I fully agree with most naturalists that all of them have descended from one species of rock pigeon: the common rock pigeon, *Columba livia*. My reasons for this belief apply to other cases too, so I will briefly give them.

If the breeds have not all descended from *C. livia*, they must have descended from at least seven or eight ancestor species. These supposed species must all have been rock pigeons—that is, they did not willingly perch or breed on trees but lived on ledges or on the ground, as domesticated pigeons do. But besides *C. livia*, only two or three other species of rock pigeons are known. They have none of the features of the domestic breeds.

The common rock pigeon, *Columba livia*, ancestor of all domestic pigeon breeds.

"It is much more likely that all domestic pigeon breeds are descended from the single known species of rock pigeon."

This means that all of the supposed ancestor species of our domestic breeds either became extinct in the wild, or they still exist in the countries where they were originally domesticated. Yet no such species are known to science. Did they become extinct? Birds that breed on ledges and are good fliers are unlikely to be exterminated. *C. livia*, the rock pigeon that has the same habits as the domestic breeds, still exists. It seems very rash to think that many similar species have been exterminated. It is much more likely that all domestic pigeon breeds are descended from the single known species of rock pigeon.

Consider also some facts in regard to the coloring of pigeons. *C. livia* is slate blue, with a white rump, white edges on some feathers, and a black bar at the end of the tail. These marks do not occur together in any other species of wild pigeon. In every one of the domestic breeds, however, all those marks sometimes occur perfectly. And the marks can appear in the offspring of birds of two different domestic breeds, even when the parents are not blue and have none of the marks.

I crossed some white fantails with some black barbs. Their offspring were mottled brown and black. I crossed these together, and one grandchild of the pure white fantail and pure black barb had as beautiful a blue color, with the white rump, white-edged feathers, and black bar, as any wild *C. livia*! We know that offspring sometimes show the characters of their ancestors. But the case of my pigeon makes sense only if all the domestic breeds have descended from the ancestor that has those features: *C. livia*.

Pigeons have been watched, and tended with the utmost care, and loved by many people. They have been domesticated for thousands of years in several parts of the world. They are listed on a menu from ancient Egypt. The ancient Roman historian Pliny wrote of

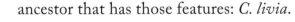

An 1837 painting of an English carrier pigeon. *On the Origin of Species* draws on Darwin's experience in breeding this and other types of pigeons.

immense prices paid for pigeons. The birds were also valued by an Indian ruler around the year 1600. Kings in other countries sent him rare pigeons, and a court historian wrote: "His Majesty by crossing the breeds . . . has improved them astonishingly." This high degree of interest in pigeons and their breeding explains the immense amount of variation we see in them.

When I first kept pigeons, I found it hard to believe that their many varieties could all have descended from the same parent species. Any naturalist could find it equally hard to believe that the many species of wild finches, or other large groups of birds, shared a single origin. Yet if the varieties of domesticated pigeons come from a single origin, could not related species of birds in nature be descended from a common parent?

The Power of Selection

One of the most remarkable features of domesticated plants and animals is that they are adapted not to their own good, but to man's use or fancy.

When we compare the cart horse and the racehorse, the various breeds of sheep that are adapted to farms or mountain pastures, and the many breeds of dogs that are useful in different ways, we must look beyond the variations that occur in nature. All these breeds were not suddenly produced as perfect and as useful as we now see them.

The key is man's power of selection that builds up differences over time. Nature gives variations, and man adds them up in directions that are useful to him. Breeders and growers do this by paying the closest attention to even the smallest variations.

The great power of selection is known. Several of our top breeders have, in a single lifetime, modified or changed breeds of cattle and sheep. Breeders speak of an animal's form as something they can model. In the German region

Dating from around 1900, this illustration of horse breeds shows some of the variety that Darwin used to explain selective breeding.

1. Арабская Л.   2. Англонорманская Л.   3. Першеронъ.

4. Бельгійская Л.   5. Шведскіе пони.   6. Венгерская Л.   7. Шотландскіе пони.   8. Іоркширская Л.

9. Ольденбургская Л.   10. Тракененская Л.   11. Англійская чистокровная Л.

of Saxony, merino sheep are highly valued. There the principle of selection is so well known that men follow it as a trade. The sheep are placed on a table and studied, like a picture by an art lover. The sheep are marked and classed, so that the very best may be selected for breeding.

Unconscious Selection

Breeders today try by careful selection to make a new strain or sub-breed better than any that exists. Even more important, though, is a different kind of selection. It may be called unconscious selection. It results from every grower or breeder trying to have the best individual animals.

Over centuries, unconscious selection would improve and modify any breed, just as modern breeders have improved their cattle within a single lifetime. One example is the English racehorse. By unconscious selection first, and then by methodical selection, English racehorses have become faster and larger than the Arab horses that were their ancestors.

In plants, we see the same gradual process of improvement. Today's roses and dahlias are larger and more beautiful than older varieties or their parent stocks. No one would ever expect to get a first-rate dahlia from the seed of a wild plant. I have seen people greatly surprised by the wonderful skill of gardeners who have produced such splendid new varieties of these flowers. The art, however, has been simple, and followed almost unconsciously.

Gardeners have cultivated the best varieties known to them and sown their seeds. When a slightly better variety happened to appear, they chose it—and so on. The gardeners of ancient Rome, who cultivated the best pear they could find, never imagined what splendid pears we should eat today. Still, we owe our excellent fruit in part to their choosing and preserving the best varieties they could find.

Man's power of selection works best when it has a high degree of variation to work on. Because useful or pleasing variations happen only occasionally, the chance of finding them will be greater if a breeder or gardener can keep a large number of individuals. One writer noted that the sheep in a certain part of England "generally belong to poor people . . . in small lots," so they never can be improved. On the other hand, nurserymen who raise large quantities of the same plants are generally far more successful than amateur gardeners in getting new and valuable varieties.

Variability is governed by many unknown laws, and the final result is infinitely complex. But I am convinced that artificial selection by man is by far the greatest power in creating domestic breeds of plants and animals.

"Man's power of selection works best when it has a high degree of variation to work on."

Eight modern varieties of pears.

CHAPTER TWO

Drawing Borders between Species

The last chapter looked at the domesticated plants and animals that people have created through selection. Now we shall see how selection applies to plants and animals in their wild state.

For selection to apply to organisms in a state of nature, variations must occur in wild species. On this subject I should give a long list of dry facts, but I will save these for my future work. For now it is enough to consider how individual plants and animals differ from one another, and where the borders between species are drawn.

Species or Variety?

No one definition of "species" has satisfied all naturalists, yet every naturalist knows vaguely what he means when he speaks of a species. A "variety" within

Darwin knew that his theory had to explain how species of plants and animals arose in "their wild state," represented here by Yosemite National Park.

a species is almost equally hard to define. Still, no one thinks that all individuals of a species are exactly the same. Even among the offspring of the same parents, many slight individual differences appear. These individual differences are highly important. They are the materials of natural selection.

I am convinced that the most experienced naturalist would be surprised at the number of variations that I have collected over the years. Even important parts of an organism's structure can show variability. For example, I would never have expected that the branching arrangement of an insect's nerves would vary within the same species. Quite recently, though, a naturalist showed that the main nerves of a **scale insect** show so much variability that they might be compared with the irregular branches of a tree.

Scale insects live on plant sap and are often found as pests on citrus fruit.

Authors sometimes argue in a circle when they state that important features of organisms never vary. That is because these same authors think that the important features *are* the ones that do not vary. Under this point of view, no variation in an important feature will ever be found! Under any other point of view, many examples can be found. Variation can occur in any part of a plant or animal.

The Wide Door of Doubt

It can be quite difficult to decide whether to call a given life-form a variety of a species or a separate species. When a naturalist can link two different forms by a series of other forms with in-between features, he treats one of those two forms as a variety of the other. He may call the more common one the species and the less common one a variety. Or the one that was first described by science is the species, and the one described later is the variety.

Often a form is called a variety because an observer thinks that links between it and a known species *might* once have existed, or *might* exist somewhere—even if those links have not been discovered. This opens a wide door for doubt and guesswork to enter.

Varieties of this doubtful nature are common. A surprising number of plants in Great Britain, France, and the United States have been called species by one botanist but varieties by another botanist. In the same way, many birds and insects in North America and Europe have been labeled species by one leading naturalist, while another ranks them as varieties—or, as they are often called, geographical races!

Many years ago, I compared birds from the separate islands of the Galápagos island group with one another and also with birds from the nearest mainland of South America. I saw other naturalists compare them as well. I was much struck by the completely vague and unscientific distinction between species and varieties. Another example is our British red grouse. Several experienced ornithologists consider it only a variety or race of a Norwegian species. Most ornithologists, however, consider the red grouse to be a definite species found only in Great Britain.

Many naturalists call two forms separate species when there is a wide distance between their homes. But what distance is enough? If the distance between America and Europe is enough to make similar forms into separate species, what about the distance from mainland Europe to Ireland?

We must admit that many forms of plants and animals called varieties by good judges could equally well be called species by other good judges. But to discuss whether they are rightly called species or varieties, without any generally accepted definition of these terms, is vainly to beat the air.

The Young Naturalist

Imagine that you are a young naturalist. You are just starting to study a group of organisms that are quite unknown to you—snails, for example.

At first, no doubt, you will be much perplexed. You will see differences from one snail to another, but you will not know what they mean. Which differences mark separate species? Which are simply signs of different varieties of the same

A small ground finch, one of the species Darwin saw in the Galápagos Islands. See "Darwin's Famous Finches" in Chapter Eleven for more about Darwin and the finches of the Galápagos.

Scientists were surprised by DNA studies suggesting that giraffes are not a single species. More research will determine how many species exist.

Lumpers and Splitters

Darwin wrote about the challenge of deciding whether two organisms belonged to different species or to varieties of the same species. Biologists still wrestle with that challenge, and they sometimes disagree about how a particular plant or animal should be labeled.

Suppose a biologist compares two groups of related plants or animals. Each group is very similar to the other, but there are some differences between them. Is each group a species? Or is one group a subspecies or a variety within the other species? The answer may depend on whether that biologist is a "lumper" or a "splitter." When in doubt, lumpers tend to bundle organisms into the same category, if the differences between them are small. They focus on the features that the organisms have in common. But splitters, when in doubt, tend to place organisms in separate groups based on their differences.

Today's biologists have a tool that Darwin didn't have: genetics, the scientific study of how genes made up of DNA inside cells carry features from parents to offspring. Each species has its own genome, or DNA blueprint. In 2016, for example, researchers looked at DNA in skin samples of 190 giraffes from many parts of Africa. All populations of giraffes have long been thought to belong to a single species, *Giraffa camelopardalis*, with as many as eleven subspecies—but the new DNA study suggested that giraffes are actually four distinct species and one subspecies.

More work is needed to confirm this finding before the scientific community accepts it, but the decision has real-world importance. Two of the currently recognized giraffe subspecies exist in such small numbers that if they are reclassified as separate species, they will instantly be recognized as endangered and will need protection.

Genetics can measure degrees of difference, but the lumper-splitter problem remains. Biologists still don't agree on how *much* difference it takes to separate two species.

species? At this point, you know nothing about how much variation exists in the world of snails.

If you focus on one group of snails—say, those with striped shells—from a single country, you will soon make up your mind how to rank most forms. You will tend to identify many separate species, because you will be impressed with how much difference you see in the snails you are continually studying. You will not yet know enough about snails in other groups and other countries to correct your first impressions.

But suppose that, as time goes on, you observe many types of snails from all over the world. In the end, you will make up your own mind about which are varieties and which are species. Your conclusions, though, will often be disputed by other naturalists.

From a Variety to a Species

Certainly no clear line has yet been drawn between species and subspecies (the forms that come very near to, but do not quite reach, the rank of species). In the same way, no clear line exists between subspecies and varieties. These stages of difference blend into one another in an unbroken series.

Little differences among individual plants or animals are of high importance for my theory. They are the first step toward varieties so small that they are barely recorded in works on natural history. As for varieties that have become distinct and permanent, I look at them as steps leading to subspecies, and subspecies as steps leading to new species.

Not all varieties reach the rank of species. They may become extinct, or they may endure as varieties for very long periods. If a variety flourished so much that it outnumbered its parent species, the variety would then rank as the species, and the parent species

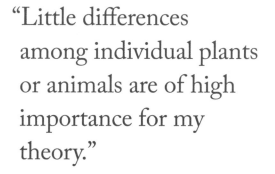

"Little differences among individual plants or animals are of high importance for my theory."

Examples of corn, or maize, from Latin America. Some types of corn are considered varieties. Others are classified as subspecies. As different as they are from one another—and from modern commercially farmed corn—they all belong to the same species, *Zea mays*.

would rank as a variety. Another possibility is that the variety might replace and exterminate the parent species. Finally, both might exist together, ranked as independent species. I shall say more on this subject in later chapters.

There appears to be a relationship among varieties, species, and genera (the plural of "genus"). In any given region, if a genus contains more than the average number of species, those species have more than the average number of varieties. In large genera, the species are apt to be closely but unevenly related, forming little clusters around certain species. Geography also plays a role. Species that are very closely related to other species seem to have restricted ranges.

In all these ways, the relationship between genera and species is like the relationship between species and subspecies, and between subspecies and varieties. We can clearly understand why this is so, if species started as varieties of other species, then grew distinct enough to be considered as separate species. These patterns are impossible to explain if each species appeared independently, with no relationships of shared ancestry linking it to other species.

The range of a species is the total area in which it occurs naturally.

Levels and Labels

Each species has a two-part scientific name. The first part is its genus, a category that can include more than one species. The second part identifies the particular species. For example, *Tyto alba* is the scientific name of the common barn owl. *Tyto* refers to a genus that includes almost all kinds of barn owls, but *alba* refers only to the common barn owl. (Most species names are in Latin, the first widespread language of science.)

The barn owl's two-part species name is part of its classification, its place in the overall world of living things. In Darwin's time, scientists classified living things using the Linnaean system, named for Carl Linnaeus, an eighteenth-century Swedish naturalist.

Linnaean classification starts with large groups, such as the kingdoms of animals, plants, and fungi. All organisms within a kingdom share certain very general features. The kingdom is broken into smaller groups called phyla, based on differences. Phyla in

Barn owl.

turn are divided into still smaller groups, and so on down to genus and species. Each level is contained within the level above it.

A family can contain one genus or many genera. A genus can contain many species or just one. A genus has a single species in it when all others have become extinct, or when the species has no close relatives.

Because a species cannot exist without a genus, and a genus cannot exist without a family, scientists can view a single species as the sole representative of its genus and its family. The Albany pitcher plant, for example, is the only species in its genus *(Cephalotus)* and family (Cephalotaceae).

From kingdom to species, the barn owl's Linnaean classification looks like this:

Kingdom: Animalia (animals)
Phylum: Chordata (animals with spinal nerve cords down the back)
Subphylum: Vertebrata (animals whose spinal cords are inside bony spines)
Class: Aves (birds)
Order: Strigiformes (owls)
Family: Tytonidae (barn owls)
Genus: *Tyto* (all barn owls except bay owls)
Species: *alba* (common barn owl)

Species names are essential to any scientific conversation about living things, and some of the other Linnaean terms are still used. Today, however, many biologists choose a classification system based on something unknown to Linnaeus. That system is called phylogenetics.

Phylogenetics, like Darwin's theory, is

In this 1737 painting, naturalist Carl Linnaeus wears the clothing of Lapland, a region of northern Sweden. He holds a plant called twinflower that is named for him—its scientific name is *Linnaea borealis*.

based on evolutionary history. It traces the genetic connections between ancestors and descendants in both living and extinct species. In phylogenetic classification, animals and plants are grouped into clusters called clades. All organisms within a clade share a common ancestor. A clade can be large-scale (such as all animals with backbones) or small-scale (such as all barn owls).

Life on Earth is like a huge tree, with branches that split into smaller branches and eventually into millions of tiny twigs, or species. As scientists learn more about similarities and differences among living things, the way they classify life may change, but the structure of groups branching into smaller groups will remain.

CHAPTER THREE

The Struggle for Life

How do varieties of plants and animals, which I have called "species in the making," become distinct species? How do groups of related species arise? We shall see in this chapter and the next that these results follow from the struggle for life.

Many individuals are born to each species, but only a small number can survive. In the struggle for life, any variation that helps an individual plant or animal succeed will keep that individual alive to reproduce—and pass on the variation to its offspring. Those offspring will gain the same improved chance to survive and reproduce. Each slight useful variation is passed on to the next generation. I have called this principle natural selection.

We have seen that artificial selection by man can produce great results. Natural selection, as we shall see, is a power immeasurably greater than man's feeble efforts.

Plants and animals are exquisitely adapted to their conditions of life and to

"We behold the face of nature bright with gladness," Darwin wrote—then explained that gladness is only part of the picture.

> "The struggle for existence is not just the struggle of the individual plant or animal to live."

one another. We see beautiful adaptations in the humblest parasite that clings to the hairs of an animal or the feathers of a bird. We see them in the structure of the beetle diving through the water, and in the plumed dandelion seed carried on the gentlest breeze. In short, we see beautiful adaptations everywhere and in every part of the organic world. How have all those adaptations been perfected?

We behold the face of nature bright with gladness. We do not see, or we forget, that the birds singing around us mostly live on insects or seeds, and are thus constantly destroying life. We forget how many of these songsters, or their eggs, or their nestlings, are destroyed by birds and beasts of prey. We do not always bear in mind that though food may be now plentiful, it is not so at all seasons of the year. Yet unless we are aware of the universal struggle for life, the whole economy of nature—every fact connected with the rarity, abundance, extinction, and variation of living things—will be only dimly seen, or quite misunderstood.

I mean "struggle for existence" in a large sense. Two wolves in a time of little food may struggle with each other to see which one shall get food and live. But a plant on the edge of a desert is said to struggle against drought, because its life depends upon moisture. A plant that produces a thousand seeds each year may be said to struggle with all the other plants that cover the ground where its seeds must try to take life. The struggle for existence is not just the struggle of the individual plant or animal to live. More important is that plant's or animal's success in leaving offspring.

The World Would Not Hold Them

The struggle for existence is unavoidable. It stems from the high rate at which plants and animals increase their numbers. More individuals are produced than can possibly survive, so there must always be a struggle for existence. This applies to the whole animal and plant kingdoms.

All species cannot keep increasing in numbers, for the world would not hold them. Every form of life increases at so high a rate that if all offspring escaped destruction, the Earth would soon be covered by the descendants of a single pair. If a plant produced only two seeds a year—most plants produce more—and each of their seedlings produced two seeds in the following years, in twenty years there would be a million plants. The only difference between organisms that produce thousands of eggs or seeds each year and those that produce only a few is that the **slow breeders** would take a few more years to populate a whole district.

In a state of nature almost every plant produces seeds. Among animals there are very few that do not mate each year. Plants and animals would most rapidly fill every place where they could exist, if their tendency to increase were not **checked** by destruction at some point.

Checks and Limits

Each species tends to increase in number, but that tendency is checked by forces working against increase. These forces are most obscure. We do not know exactly what all the checks are in even a single species. I will make only a few remarks on some general points.

Among animals, eggs or the very young seem to suffer the most destruction, although this is not always so. With plants, there is a vast destruction of seeds. Seedlings or very young plants also suffer when sprouting in ground that is already thickly stocked with other plants, and they are destroyed in vast numbers by various enemies.

I marked all the seedlings of our native weeds as they came up on a piece of ground three feet long and two wide, dug and cleared, where there could be no choking from other plants. Out of the 357 plants that came up, 295 were destroyed, chiefly by slugs and insects. On another plot of ground three feet by four, twenty species grew, but nine perished from the other species growing up freely.

The amount of food available for each species sets the upper limit to which

Slow breeders include animals such as elephants and whales, which carry their young for many months before giving birth, usually to just one infant.

By "checked" Darwin meant "blocked" or "limited."

A weasel steals a bird's eggs.

it can increase. Being eaten by others, though, frequently sets the size of a population. One example is the game birds and animals on English estates. Hundreds of thousands of them are shot each year, but shooting is not the only thing that can limit the size of their populations. Vermin such as rats, which devour young birds and animals, are a bigger check than human hunters, which is why humans take pains to destroy vermin.

Suppose that not one game bird or animal were shot for twenty years, and also that no vermin were destroyed during the same time. At the end of twenty years there would most likely be less game than at present, not more, because the vermin would have destroyed more game birds and animals than would have been killed by human hunters.

On the other hand, beasts of prey destroy few or even no individuals of some species, such as the elephant and rhinoceros. Even the tiger in India rarely dares to attack a young elephant protected by its mother.

Climate plays an important part in determining the size of a population. I believe that seasons of extreme cold or drought are the most effective of all checks. I estimated that the exceptionally severe winter of 1854–55 destroyed four-fifths, or 80 percent, of the birds in my own grounds. This is a tremendous destruction when we remember that among humans, 10 percent is considered an extraordinarily severe rate of death from epidemics of disease.

One way that climate checks the increase of species is by reducing the amount of available food. This brings on a severe struggle among all individuals that eat the same food, whether they belong to the same or different species. Although locusts and goats belong to widely different species, for example, they may compete for the grasses that both of them eat. But the struggle almost always will be greatest among individuals of the same species. They live in the same places, require the same food, and face the same dangers.

Climate also acts directly on organisms. In cases of extreme cold, the least vigorous organisms, or those that have had the least food, will suffer most.

Game birds and animals are species that humans hunt for sport or for food, such as pheasants and deer.

The rare, elusive snow leopard is superbly adapted to life in extremely cold regions. A camera trap caught this scene in Mongolia.

When we reach the Arctic regions, or snow-capped summits, or absolute deserts, the struggle for life is almost entirely with the elements.

Disease is another check on the increase of populations. A species living in highly favorable conditions may increase greatly in a small area. When this happens, epidemics of disease often appear and spread through the population. This check on population increase is apart from the struggle of individuals with one another.

Battle within Battle

Nature is full of complex and unexpected relationships among the living things that must struggle together in the same place. I will give only one example. It is simple, but it has interested me.

My father-in-law's property in Staffordshire contains a large and extremely barren heath that had never been touched by the hand of man. Twenty-five years earlier, however, several hundred acres of exactly the same kind of heath had been fenced and planted with Scotch fir trees. The change in the vegetation of this fir plantation was remarkable.

A heath is a tract of uncultivated land with few or no trees, although grasses and small shrubs may grow there.

Not only had the population sizes of the heath plants wholly changed in the fir plantation, but twelve new species of plants flourished there that could not be found on the untouched heath. The effect on the insects must have been still greater. Six insect-eating birds were very common in the plantation but were not seen on the heath, although two or three other insect-eating birds were found there. Here we see the powerful change made by introducing a single tree species, the Scotch fir. The only other difference is that the plantation was fenced to keep cattle out.

Fencing is an important element in the struggle for existence. I plainly saw this in another area of extensive heaths, with a few clumps of old Scotch firs on the distant hilltops. Within the last ten years, large spaces of these heaths have been fenced. Firs are now springing up in multitudes, so close together that all cannot live.

When I learned that these had not been planted by man, but had sprung up naturally, I was much surprised at their numbers. I went to several viewpoints from which I could see hundreds of acres of unfenced heath. I could not see a single Scotch fir on the unfenced heath, except the old hilltop clumps. But when I looked closely between the stems of the heath plants in this unfenced area, I found a multitude of Scotch fir seedlings and little trees that had been constantly eaten down by cattle.

In one square yard of heath, about a hundred yards from one of the old clumps, I counted thirty-two little trees. One of them, judging from its growth rings, had

Darwin spent hours counting trees and seedlings to see how fences and cattle had changed heath land such as this.

been trying for twenty-six years to raise its head above the stems of the heath—and failed. No wonder that as soon as part of the heath was fenced to keep out the grazing cattle, it became thickly clothed with vigorously growing young firs.

Most natural relationships are not as simple as this. Battle within battle must ever be going on, yet in the long run the forces are so well balanced that the face of nature remains the same for long periods of time.

A bumblebee feeds on the nectar of red clover.

Clover and Cats

Clover and cats are another example of plants and animals bound together by a web of complex relations.

Many plants depend on insects to **fertilize** them. My own experiments have shown that bumblebees are almost essential to the fertilizing of wild pansy and some kinds of clovers. Red clover can be fertilized *only* by **bumblebees**, because other insects cannot reach its nectar. This suggests that if bumblebees became very rare, or extinct, the wild pansy and red clover would also become very rare, or disappear.

The number of bumblebees in any area depends greatly on the number of field mice, because mice destroy the bees' honeycombs and nests. And as everyone knows, the number of mice depends largely on the number of cats.

One observer has pointed out that honeycombs and bees' nests are more common near towns than out in the countryside, because people in towns keep cats. More cats mean fewer mice, and fewer mice mean more bees. More bees, in turn, mean more fertilizing of certain plants. Communities that have a lot of cats could well have more wild pansy and red clover nearby than other communities.

Insects fertilize plants by carrying pollen from one plant to another while they feed on the nectar, or sweet juice, inside flowers.

In his original text, Darwin used the word "humble-bee," an old name for the bumblebee.

Cats indirectly help bees by killing hive-destroying mice.

Every species faces limits at different stages of its growth, in different seasons, or in different locations. One or two of these limits might be more powerful than the rest, but together they determine the average number of individuals that survive—or even whether the species continues to exist.

When we look at the plants and bushes on an entangled bank of vegetation, we may think that the variety of species, and the number of each species, is due to chance. But how false a view this is! The tangle of plants is the outcome of interactions among a host of living things.

If a forest is cut down, a very different vegetation springs up. Fast-growing weeds, wildflowers, and saplings are the first to appear. Large, slow-growing trees take generations to reappear. In the southeastern United States, Indians cleared land centuries ago to build their earthen mounds—yet today the forests on some mounds are identical to the surrounding forests of mature trees. This means that the vegetation upon those mounds must have changed slowly, passing through many stages.

What a struggle must have taken place on the mounds during the long centuries as the different kinds of trees each scattered their seeds by the thousands every year. What war among insects, snails, birds and beasts of prey, and other animals, all striving to increase, all feeding on one another, or on the trees and their seeds and seedlings, or on the other plants that first choked the ground, until the mounds were covered with mature forests.

Throw a handful of feathers into the air, and all of them must fall to the ground according to laws of physics. Knowing how each feather will fall is a simple problem compared to the action and reaction of the countless plants and animals that shaped, over centuries, the forests now growing on the old Indian ruins!

The Complex Web

The structure of every living thing is related to every other living thing with which it competes, or from which it must escape, or on which it preys. We see this interconnected web in the teeth and talons of the tiger, adapted to help it seize and tear its prey. We see it also in the legs and claws of the tiny parasite that clings to a hair on the tiger's body.

Yet we do not easily see *all* the ways in which a living thing's structure is related to the other lives around it. When we look at the beautifully plumed seed of the dandelion, or the flattened and fringed legs of the water beetle, we see that they are adapted to help the seed float on the air and the beetle dive through the water.

If we consider these benefits in greater detail, we discover that they are closely interconnected with everything around the dandelion and the beetle.

The advantage of the dandelion's plumed seeds is greatest where the land is already thickly covered with other plants. Seeds that float far and high have a chance of being widely spread, so that some of them may fall on unoccupied ground. And the water beetle's legs, so well adapted for diving, allow it to compete for prey with other water insects, and also to escape becoming prey itself.

It is good to try to imagine the advantage that any feature or form gives to the plant or animal that has it. This will convince us of our ignorance on the complex relations among organic beings. All we can do is keep steadily in mind that each living thing is striving to increase, and that each—at some time of its life, or season of the year—must struggle for life.

A diving beetle on an underwater hunt.

These dandelion seeds will float on the next breeze.

CHAPTER FOUR

Survival of the Fittest

The struggle for existence was the subject of the last chapter. Now, how will that struggle act on the natural variation that occurs in all species of living things?

We saw in Chapter One that the principle of selection is a powerful tool in the hands of man. Can that same tool—selection—operate in nature, without the guiding hand of man? I think we shall see that it can.

Bear in mind the strange peculiarities of individual variation, and the strength of heredity. Remember also the infinitely complex and close-fitting relationships of all living things to one another and to the environment in which they live. We know that variations useful to humans have occurred. It is certain that other variations—changes useful not to humans but to

Ama Dablam, a peak in the Himalayan mountain range. Darwin explained how barriers such as mountain ranges can keep species from migrating into new areas.

English biologist and philosopher Herbert Spencer (1820–1903) coined the phrase "survival of the fittest" as an alternative to Darwin's "natural selection." Darwin added the phrase to the *Origin of Species* in 1868. It means "best adapted to survive in the local environment."

organisms in the great and complex battle of life—have naturally occurred in the course of thousands of generations.

Now remember that many more individuals are born than can possibly survive. If useful variations naturally occur, can we doubt that individuals with even a small advantage over others would have the best chance of surviving and reproducing? On the other hand, we may feel sure that any harmful variation would be destroyed. This preservation of favorable variations and rejection of harmful ones is what I call natural selection.

Silent and Invisible Work

Natural selection is best seen in a country undergoing some physical change—for instance, of climate. If a country were to grow warmer or colder, some species would increase, some would decrease, and some might become extinct. Because we have seen the close and complex ways that the species in a region are bound together, we know that any change in the number of some species would affect many other species, apart from the change of climate itself.

If the country were easy to enter, new species better adapted to the warmer or colder climate would certainly migrate into it. This would further disturb the relations of the original inhabitants, because even a single kind of tree or mammal can have a powerful influence when it enters a place where it did not exist before.

But new and better-adapted forms could not freely enter an island, or a country surrounded by barriers. In that case, some of the original inhabitants might change over time, adapting to the new warmer or colder conditions. Every small modification that arose in the course of ages, if it better fitted individuals to their changed climate, would be passed on to generations of offspring. Natural selection would have free scope for improvement.

Unless favorable variations occur, natural selection can do nothing. Yet I do not believe that an extreme amount of variability is necessary. Man can certainly produce great results by adding up small individual differences. Nature could

A bark beetle is nearly invisible on a tree. Scientists now use the term "cryptic coloration" for adaptations that help creatures "disappear" into their backgrounds.

do the same, but far more easily, because nature has incomparably longer time in which to work. Man selects only for his own good. Nature selects only for the good of the being which she tends. How fleeting are the wishes and efforts of man! How short his time! And for that reason how poor his products will be, compared with those built up by nature during whole geological periods.

Every hour of every day, throughout the world, natural selection studies every variation, even the slightest. It rejects that which is bad. It preserves and adds up all that is good. Silently and invisibly, natural selection works whenever and wherever it can to better fit each type of organic being to its conditions of life. We see nothing of these slow changes until the hand of time has marked the long lapse of ages. Even then, our view into past geological time is imperfect. We see only that the forms of life around us are different from what they once were.

Natural selection acts only for the good of each being, acting on characters and structures that we may not think are important. Consider the color of an insect or bird. We see that leaf-eating insects are green, and bark feeders are spotted gray. Each is colored to match the surface on which it spends its time. The alpine ptarmigan, a bird that dwells in high places, is white in winter to blend with the snows. In contrast, the black grouse is the color of the peaty earth on which it lives. We must believe that these tints help the insects and birds by preserving them from predators.

Darwin could have meant the white-tailed ptarmigan, which is found only in North America, or the rock ptarmigan, which is found in Eurasia and North America. Both are birds of alpine habitat. They are found above the tree line on mountains and in tundras and forests near the Arctic. Both have white feathers during the winter.

A Swifter Wolf

I will give an imaginary example to make it clear how natural selection acts. Let us take the case of a wolf that preys on various animals. It catches some by stealth, some by strength, and some by speed. Now suppose that just when the wolf needs food most, its fastest prey, a deer, increases in numbers. Another possibility is that the other, slower prey animals decrease. Either way, the swiftest wolves would have the best chance of surviving, because they would be best at catching deer, a plentiful food source. These swift wolves would be preserved, or selected.

Even if the numbers of our wolf's prey did not increase or decrease, a wolf pup might be born with a tendency to pursue certain kinds of prey. We know this to be true of cats. One cat takes to catching rats, while another pursues mice. One catches birds, while another catches rabbits. Cats are known to pass to their kittens the tendency to hunt rats rather than mice.

So if a wolf pup were born with a tendency to pursue deer, and if that tendency helped it in any way, that wolf would have the best chance of surviving and having pups of its own. Some of them would probably inherit the same tendency. Repetition over generations might give rise to a new variety of unusually fast wolf, one that was especially good at hunting deer. This variety would either live side-by-side with the parent-form of wolf, or replace it.

I have been told that a real-life example exists in the Catskill Mountains in the United

Wolves in winter.

Natural Selection in the Twenty-First Century

Charles Darwin and fellow naturalist Alfred Russel Wallace were the first to describe the *how* of evolution—or, as Darwin called it, "descent with modification." Working separately, they came up with the same mechanism by which new species arise through changes in old ones.

Darwin called that mechanism "natural selection" and explained it in the *Origin*. He saw selection as the engine of evolution. This includes sexual selection, which is a specific type of natural selection. Sexual selection modifies and improves features that help organisms find, attract, or compete for mates. The elaborate tail of a male bird of paradise and the female's preference for such a tail are both results of sexual selection.

Today scientists are still studying the complex operations of selection. They have also learned more about other forces that drive evolution. Some important ones are mutation, gene flow, and genetic drift.

A mutation is a change in an organism's DNA, the genetic material within cells. Mutations can occur when a cell divides to become two cells. If the DNA fails to copy correctly, the result is a mutation. Outside forces such as radiation can also cause mutations. Not all mutations are passed to offspring, but if they occur in the DNA of reproductive cells, they are inherited by the next generation. Mutations are random. They may help or harm the organism and its offspring. They may also have no effect on its fitness and survival.

Gene flow is the movement of new genetic material into a population. One example occurs in Alaska when domestic caribou escape and join wild caribou herds, mixing their gene pools. Gene flow also takes place when bees or breezes carry pollen from the flowers in one yard to the flowers in a yard five blocks away. Gene flow increases the genetic variety within a population, creating more raw material for natural selection.

Genetic drift is random change in the genetic makeup of a population. It can be the result of luck or chance—some individuals simply leave more descendants than others, so their traits increase. Genetic drift can happen quickly when a population suddenly becomes much smaller. Examples include a large herd of elephants reduced to a few individuals by illegal hunting, or a single grove of trees left standing after a forest fire. These individuals' traits would increase within their populations, not because natural selection "chose" them for their adaptations, but because there is less overall genetic variety.

A rare genetic mutation made this grasshopper bright pink instead of the usual green.

Conditions such as climate, habitat loss, changes in an environment, or even an accident can also split a species into separate groups. Millions of years ago, for example, some ancient ancestors of monkeys found their way from Africa to South America, probably carried on floating vegetation. The South American and African monkey populations could no longer share genetic material. Entirely different families of monkeys evolved in the two continents.

States, where there are two varieties of wolf. One is lightly built, with a shape like that of a racing greyhound. It pursues deer. The other is more bulky, with shorter legs. It more often attacks flocks of sheep.

Place and Time

What circumstances are most favorable or unfavorable to natural selection? Where and how will new forms of life be most likely to appear?

I conclude that the places most favorable for producing many new forms of life will be large continental areas that undergo many changes over millions of years. Forces within the Earth, such as the movements that lift mountain ranges, will raise the land—and eventually may lower it again. When seas rise, they will cover much of the land. While the sea level is high, the large continental area will spend long periods split up into islands. When the sea level falls, the islands will once again become parts of a large continent.

When the area exists as a continent, it will be inhabited by numerous species. When it is changed into islands, individuals of a given species will exist on each island, but they will no longer be able to interbreed with those from other islands. Whenever a variation or new modification occurs on one island, it will spread through the island, but not beyond it. Because few or no plants and animals will come from outside, empty **places** in each island will in time be filled by new adaptations of the old inhabitants.

When the islands are once again joined into a continent, large numbers of individuals and species will be thrown together, and competition will become severe. The most improved species will spread. Those less improved may become extinct. The number of each species in the new continent will change relative to the numbers of other species. All these changes will give rise to new opportunities. They will create a fair field for natural selection to improve the inhabitants still further, and produce new species.

Natural selection will always act with extreme slowness. It will depend upon there being places in the **economy of nature** that can be better filled by newly modified or adapted forms of species than by the old forms that already exist. Such places are often created by the very slow physical changes in the environment that I have just described. Barriers such as mountain ranges or large rivers

By "place" Darwin meant what scientists now call a "niche." It is the role that a species fills in its setting— how it finds food and shelter, reproduces, and interacts with other organisms.

Darwin used the phrase "economy of nature" (or "polity of nature") to mean the total of all relationships among organisms and their environment, similar to the modern term "ecology."

may also create niches and keep outside forms from coming in to fill them.

Most of all, natural selection will depend on the modification of some species through variation, which is apparently always a slow process. It is slower still if individuals with a modification are able to interbreed with those from outside their range or with new arrivals, rather than always interbreeding with others that share the modification.

Located in New Mexico's Chaco Culture National Historical Park, the Menefee Formation is a series of rock layers formed over millions of years by rivers that once flowed across this part of the continent.

Many will exclaim that these reasons are enough to wholly stop the action of natural selection. I do not believe so. Natural selection will always act very slowly, often at long intervals of time, and generally on only a very few inhabitants of the same region at the same time. This slow, occasional action of natural selection fits perfectly well with what geology tells us about how the inhabitants of this world have changed over long periods of time, as I will show in Chapter Nine.

Slow though the process of selection may be, feeble humans can do much by the power of artificial selection. I can see no limit to the amount of much greater change, to the beauty and infinite complexity of the way all organic beings may adapt to one another and to their physical conditions of life, over the long course of time by nature's power of selection.

Divergence of Character

Forms that are similar grow more different over time through the action of natural selection. One effect of natural selection, in other words, is to increase the amount of difference between related forms. I call this divergence of character. It is of high importance in my theory.

Varieties are more similar to one another than species are, yet according to my view, varieties are species in the process of formation. How does the smaller difference between varieties grow into the bigger difference between species?

As has always been my practice, let us seek light from our domestic productions. Suppose that at an early period one man preferred swifter horses, but another preferred stronger and more bulky horses. The early differences would be very slight. But in the course of time, as some breeders selected swifter horses and other breeders selected stronger horses, the differences would become ever greater.

After the lapse of centuries, the two types would become two well-established and distinct breeds. Over those centuries, horses that were neither very swift nor very strong will have been neglected. They will have tended to disappear. Here we see the principle of divergence in artificial selection. It causes differences that are barely noticeable at first to become more and more noticeable, until breeds diverge, or draw apart, from one another and from their common parent.

Can the same principle apply in nature? I believe it can and does apply most efficiently, for one simple reason. Natural selection must follow the principle of divergence of character, because the more diverse or varied the descendants of any species become, the better they can seize upon many different niches in the economy of nature, and so increase in numbers.

We can clearly see this in animals with simple habits. Take the case of a meat-eating mammal such as a fox. Once the fox population in a region has grown as large as the supply of prey animals can support, the only way the number of foxes can increase is if new generations seize on niches that are already

The Clydesdale breed *(above)* **is a strong workhorse.**

This Arabian mare *(left)* **comes from a breed of horse long prized for its swiftness.**

filled by other kinds of animals. This might mean that some fox descendants feed on new kinds of prey, either dead or alive. Some might live and hunt in new ways, such as by climbing trees or prowling in swamps. Some might enlarge their diet beyond meat.

The more varied the descendants of foxes become in their structure and habits, the more niches they can occupy. And what applies to the fox will apply throughout all time to all animals and plants.

Great diversity of structure supports the greatest amount of life. In an extremely small area, especially one into which new animals and plants can freely enter, competition between individuals must be severe. In such places we always find great diversity of inhabitants.

I found that a piece of ground, three feet by four in size, exposed for many years to exactly the same conditions, supported twenty species of plants. To show how much they differed from one another, these twenty species belonged to eighteen genera and eight orders. The same high rate of diversity is found among plants and insects in isolated environments such as small islands and small freshwater ponds.

I think we may assume that the modified descendants of any species become more likely to succeed as they become more diverse. How does this principle of divergence of character combine with the principles of natural selection and extinction?

We have seen that in each country some genera contain more species than others. We have also seen that species in the larger genera most often have varieties, which are the beginnings of new species. This might have been expected. Natural selection depends upon one form having an advantage over other forms in the struggle for existence, so it will chiefly act on forms that already have some advantage. If a genus has a great many species, those species must have inherited from their shared ancestor some advantage that originally let them increase, diverge, and become independent species.

This fox kit's mother is rearing her young in a hollow tree. Foxes can climb, and Darwin thought that some might turn to hunting in trees if necessary.

Ponds such as this one—as well as other small, isolated environments that Darwin studied—are home to highly diverse populations of species.

Looking to the future, we can predict that the groups of plants and animals that now have many species and have suffered the fewest extinctions will continue to increase for a long time. No one can predict which groups will ultimately triumph, for we know that many large groups have become extinct. Yet we may predict that as the larger groups steadily increase, a multitude of smaller groups will become utterly extinct, leaving no descendants.

The Great Tree of Life

Whether natural selection has really acted in nature, changing and adapting the various forms of life, must be judged by the evidence given in the following chapters. But we already see how natural selection requires the extinction of some species, and geology plainly declares how many forms have become extinct in the world's history.

It is a truly wonderful fact that all animals and all plants throughout all time and space should be related to one another. The relationships among the various forms of life have sometimes been represented by a great tree. I believe this image largely speaks the truth. Green and budding twigs may represent

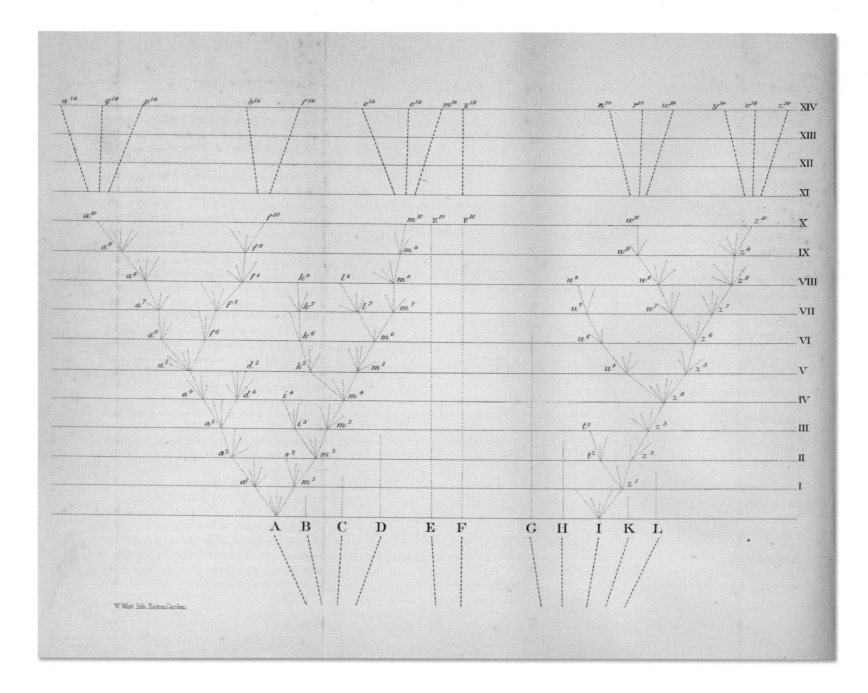

existing species. Dry twigs produced during earlier years may represent the long series of extinct species.

At each period of growth, all the growing twigs have tried to branch out on all sides, to overshadow and kill the surrounding twigs and branches, as species, genera, and families have tried to overmaster others in the great battle for life. The limbs that are now divided into great branches, which split into lesser and lesser branches, were once budding twigs, when the tree was small. This connection of old and new buds by branching limbs may well represent the classification of all extinct and living species, in groups within other groups.

Many twigs flourished when the tree was a mere bush. Now only a few of them, grown into great branches, survive and bear all the other branches. It is the same with the species that lived during long-past geological periods. Very few of them have living descendants. From the first growth of the tree, many a limb and branch has decayed and dropped off. These lost branches may represent the orders, families, and genera that have no living representatives and are known to us only from fossils.

Buds give rise to fresh buds as they grow, and these, if they are strong and healthy, branch out and overtake many feebler branches on all sides. So I believe it has been with the great Tree of Life, which fills with its dead and broken branches the crust of the Earth, and covers the surface with its ever-branching and beautiful ramifications.

Darwin's diagram of branching species was the only illustration in the first edition of the *Origin of Species*.

CHAPTER FIVE

The Horse's Stripes

We do not know what causes variation. Yet here and there we dimly catch a faint ray of light, and we feel sure that there must be some cause for each variation, however small.

I said in Chapter One that the laws governing inheritance are entirely unknown. We cannot say, for example, how a feature such as a long nose is passed from a mother to a child, or why some of that woman's children inherit her long nose but others do not. The same is true of variation in nature. Laws must govern it, but we do not grasp them. Still, the patterns of variation I will discuss in this chapter—those faint rays of light on the subject—are signs of natural selection at work.

When a variation is of the slightest use to a being, we cannot tell how much

Some species of the small rodents called lemmings live near the Arctic and are known for their thick fur. Did they inherit thick fur, Darwin wondered, or develop it because of the cold in which they live?

A Fuegian steamer duck, which Darwin called a "loggerheaded duck."

of it is due to the built-up effects of natural selection and how much is due to the conditions of life. Animals of the same species have thicker fur when they have lived in colder climates. How much of this difference is because thickly furred individuals have been favored by natural selection over many generations? How much is due to the direct action of the severe climate on those individuals, causing their fur to grow in more thickly?

I could give examples of the same variation appearing in individuals of the same species that live under entirely different conditions of life. I could also give examples of different variations appearing in individuals that live under the same conditions. This leads me to think that the conditions of life have very little weight in variation. Natural selection, however, will build up all useful variations, however small, until they become plainly developed and visible to us.

Flightless Birds

Many animals have features that can be explained by lack of use. Consider the case of a species of bird that cannot fly because its wings are too small or weak to carry it. One such species is the loggerheaded duck of South America, which can only flap along the surface of the water. It has a large body and stunted wings. The shrinking of wings in flightless birds follows what I believe to be a general principle: that natural selection always tries to be economical, to avoid waste.

Suppose a change in the conditions of life—such as migrating to an island without predators—makes a bird's wings less useful for its survival. In that new environment, every variation that produces a slightly smaller wing will be seized on by natural selection, because it benefits the bird to have less nourishment wasted in building up a useless body part.

What about a flightless bird that does not live on an island? The ostrich lives in the continent of Africa, where it faces beasts of prey. It cannot escape by flight, but it defends itself from enemies by kicking. We may imagine that as natural selection made the ostrich's body larger and heavier over many generations, its legs were used more, and its wings less, until the ostrich became incapable of flight.

Cave Dwellers

Just as some bird species have lost the power of flight, some species of animals that live underground have lost the power of sight. The eyes of moles and of some burrowing rodents are poorly developed. In some cases they are quite covered up by skin and fur. This is probably due to gradual reduction from disuse, aided perhaps by natural selection.

In South America, a burrowing rodent called the tuco-tuco is even more subterranean in its habits than the mole. I was told by someone who had often caught them that they were frequently blind. One that I kept alive was certainly blind. After it died, I determined that its blindness was caused by inflammation of the membrane that covers the eyes.

Frequent inflammation of the eyes must be harmful to any animal. Animals with subterranean habits do not absolutely need eyes. A shrinking in size of the eyes, with the eyelids sealing together and fur growing over them, might help these animals by preventing inflammation. If so, natural selection would constantly aid the effects of disuse.

The two places in the world with the most kinds of blind animals—including crabs, rats, and insects—are caves in Austria, in the center of Europe; and in Kentucky, in North America. It is difficult to imagine conditions of life more

Scalopus aquaticus, the eastern mole, lives comfortably underground with no visible eyes. Beneath its skin are poorly developed eyes that may detect light.

The camel cricket, with very long antennae, belongs to a large family of crickets adapted to cave life.

Antennae serve as feelers. Longer antennae give insects more ability to sense their surroundings.

similar than in these deep limestone caverns, which are alike in climate. If the blind animals had been separately created for the two sets of caverns, one in North America and the other in Europe, we might have expected them to be very similar. But this is not the case. Cave insects in Europe are not more closely related to North American insects than other European creatures are related to those of North America.

My theory offers a different explanation. Suppose that American animals with ordinary powers of vision slowly migrated, generation after generation, from the outer world deeper and deeper into the Kentucky caves. European animals did the same thing in the caves of Austria. We have some evidence of this. Close to the entrances of caves live animals that are not too different from ordinary forms. Further in are those constructed for twilight. Deepest of all are those destined for total darkness.

By the time a species reaches the deepest recesses of a cave, after numberless generations, disuse has more or less obliterated its eyes. Natural selection will often have brought about other changes, such as longer **antennae** in insects, making up for blindness.

Under my theory, we might expect to see connections between the American cave animals and the other animals of America, and connections between the European cave animals and the other animals of Europe. I hear that this is the case with some of the American cave animals, and some European cave insects are very closely related to insects of the surrounding country. It would be most difficult to explain this under the ordinary view that these species were all independently created.

Species and Genus

Characters found in only some species within a genus tend to vary more than the characters that are shared by *all* species in the genus.

A simple example would be a large genus containing many species of

ON THE ORIGIN OF SPECIES

flowering plants. If some species had blue flowers and some had red flowers, color would be a character at the species level, and one that is known to show variation across the genus. No one would be surprised at one of the blue species varying into red, or one of the red species varying into blue. But if all species in the genus had blue flowers, color would be a character of the entire genus. Any plant with red flowers would be more unusual.

I believe that features found in every species of a genus were inherited from a long-ago ancestor shared by the whole genus. Since then, these features have not varied, or only slightly, so they are unlikely to vary now.

A color variant stands out in a field of tulips.

The Missing Piece

Charles Darwin had a major problem when he wrote the *Origin*. Heredity was central to his argument about how new species are formed by natural selection—but neither he nor anyone else at the time knew how heredity works. They knew that offspring inherit features from their parents, but they didn't know how.

Darwin understood that heredity links children to their parents and their more distant ancestors, and that it links living species to the extinct species that were *their* ancestors.

He also understood that all living things are related, whether closely or distantly, by inheritance. Still, his carefully thought-out picture of evolution was missing one piece. He could not explain the mechanism behind the ties of inheritance.

Darwin died in 1882. In the 1890s scientists began filling in that missing piece, gradually solving the mystery of heredity. By 1905 that field of study had come to be called genetics. During the 1940s and 1950s, DNA was identified as the molecule inside cells that carries genetic information. By 2003 scientists had mapped the human genome, the complete set of genetic material that defines the human species. Today, genetics is one of the liveliest frontiers in science.

Yet a key step toward solving the mystery of heredity had been taken during Darwin's lifetime. It was the work of an Austrian monk named Gregor Mendel.

In 1865 Mendel published a paper about his experiments on pea plants. He wanted to measure the way traits such as tallness and shortness passed from one generation of plants to the next. Mendel discovered that by interbreeding tall and short pea plants—and their descendants—he could produce various combinations of tall plants and short plants, but no in-between or medium-size plants.

Mendel's results showed that inheritance did not "blend" different versions of a trait,

A German stamp bears the portrait of Gregor Mendel, monk and early researcher in genetics.

in the way that black and white paint can be blended to make gray. Instead, traits seemed to be passed from parents to offspring in distinct, unblendable packages or particles of some sort.

Those particles, as scientists discovered, are genes. They are the units of heredity, carried from one generation to the next in reproductive cells: sperm and eggs. Each cell has a nucleus, or center, that contains long chains of molecules. These chains, called chromosomes, are made of strands of DNA.

Each chromosome is divided into many regions, which are the genes. The DNA of each gene is the blueprint for part of the genome, or total genetic map of a species. Small variations in genes—caused by the way the parents' DNA combines or by mutations—create the differences we see among individuals of the same species.

We now know what Darwin didn't: how heredity works. (There is a very small chance that Darwin might have heard of Mendel's work, but if so, he did not know enough about it to realize its importance.) Once the mechanism of heredity began to be understood, however, it only strengthened Darwin's points about variation, natural selection, and the way life-forms change over time.

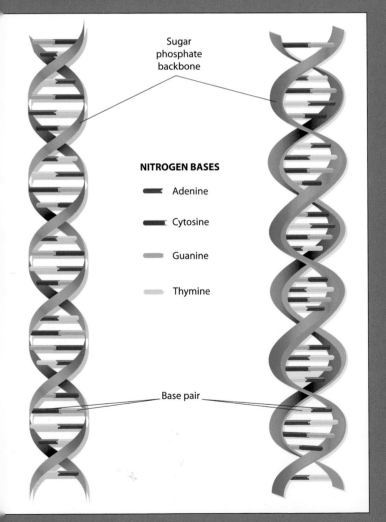

Sugar phosphate backbone

NITROGEN BASES

- Adenine
- Cytosine
- Guanine
- Thymine

Base pair

The framework of each DNA strand consists of two twisting strips of sugar phosphate, a chemical compound that conducts energy. Linking the two strips, like rungs on a ladder, are units called base pairs, each made of two compounds called nitrogen bases. Four bases combine in a multitude of ways to make up DNA.

On the other hand, features that set apart different species in the genus have varied more recently. They have appeared in the time since the species branched off from their shared ancestor. These newer features are often somewhat variable—more variable, at least, than features that have changed little or not at all for a very long period.

Zebras, Quaggas, and More

Some kinds of variation seem surprising. A variety of one species, for example, may show features found in a different, but related, species. Or a plant or animal species may show features from a distant ancestor.

I mentioned in Chapter One that domestic pigeons of all breeds, whatever their color, occasionally produce slate-blue offspring with two black bars on their wings. These are features of the wild common rock pigeon, *Columba livia*, the ancestor of all domestic pigeons. I think no one will doubt that this is a case of **reversion**.

"Reversion" means that individuals revert to, or unexpectedly show, features found in their ancestors.

If we do not know the ancestor of a group of species, we may not know whether a particular variation is a reversion to the ancestor's features. Still, by my theory we ought sometimes to find the offspring of a species showing features found in some related species. And this undoubtedly is the case in nature.

I will give one curious and complex example. It involves coloring and

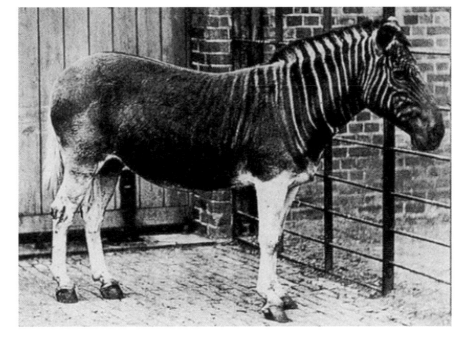

A quagga in the London Zoo, photographed in 1869.

Donkeys are domesticated descendants of the African wild ass. Two other species of wild ass live in Asia.

———

Quaggas became extinct in 1883, when the last one died in a zoo in Amsterdam.

See Chapter Eight for more about the offspring of crossbreeding between donkeys and horses.

stripes in the equids. This family includes the horse, the zebra, and several species of asses, one of which is the donkey.

Zebras have stripes on their heads, bodies, and legs. The quagga, a South African subspecies of zebra, is barred like a zebra on the body but not on the legs, although one quagga with zebralike leg stripes has been seen.

In contrast, donkeys often have distinct zebralike bars on their legs. These are most noticeable in the very young. Donkeys also frequently have a stripe along the length of the spine, and one or sometimes two stripes on the shoulder. In dark-colored animals, these stripes are sometimes very hard to see, or completely absent.

Where horses are concerned, I have collected cases in England of the spinal stripe in horses of many breeds and colors. Bars on the legs are not rare in horses of the grayish-brown color that we call dun. My son made a careful sketch for me of a dun-colored cart horse with a double stripe on each shoulder, as well as leg stripes. I have received another report of a small dun-colored pony with three short parallel stripes on each shoulder.

I have collected cases of leg and shoulder stripes in horses of very different breeds from Britain to Eastern China, and from Norway to the islands of the South China Sea. In all parts of the world, stripes are rare, but they occur most often on dun-colored horses.

What happens when the species of equids are crossbred in captivity? One expert claims that the common mule, the offspring of a donkey and a horse, is likely to have bars on its legs. I once saw a mule with its legs so much striped that anyone might have thought it was the offspring of a zebra. In hybrids between donkey and zebra, the legs are much more clearly barred than the rest of the body.

Onagers, or Asiatic wild asses, in the Negev Mountains of Israel.

In one crossing of a female horse with a male quagga, the hybrid offspring had noticeable leg stripes, although these are rare on both horses and quaggas. In another most remarkable case, a donkey was crossbred with an Asiatic wild ass. Although the donkey does not always have stripes, and the Asiatic wild ass has neither leg stripes nor shoulder stripes, their offspring had bars on all four legs, three short shoulder stripes, and even some zebralike stripes on the sides of its face.

To sum up, several distinct species of equids sometimes show stripes on the legs like a zebra, or stripes on the shoulders like an ass. In horses this tendency goes with a dun color, similar to the general coloring of all ass species. The appearance of the stripes does not go along with any other difference in form or structure. And the tendency to become striped is strongest in hybrids.

Looking back thousands on thousands of generations, I imagine an animal striped like a zebra, but perhaps otherwise very different from the modern zebra. It is the common parent of our domestic horse and of the African and Asiatic wild asses, the quagga, and the zebra. Anyone who believes that each equid species was independently created must believe that each was created with a tendency to become striped like other species. In addition, each must have been created with a strong tendency, when artificially crossed with species from distant parts of the world, to produce striped hybrids that look more like other species than like their own parents. This view, it seems to me, rejects a real cause—my theory of descent with modification by natural selection—in favor of an unreal, or at least unknown, cause.

I would almost as soon believe that fossil shells had never lived, but were created in stone to mock the shells now living on the seashore.

Our Deep Ignorance

Our ignorance of the laws of variation is profound. Not in one case out of a hundred can we pretend to know why part of a plant or animal differs from the same part in its parents.

Still, we see enough to know that there must be a cause for each slight difference between parents and their offspring. Whatever causes these differences, if the differences give the offspring an advantage in living and reproducing, they will be passed on. Natural selection steadily builds such differences into the many diverse adaptations that enable the countless beings on the face of this Earth to struggle with one another, so that the best adapted of them survive.

CHAPTER SIX

Difficulties of My Theory

By this point, difficulties and questions about my theory will have occurred to the reader. Some difficulties are so serious that I can never reflect on them without being staggered. Most of them, though, are easily solved. To the best of my judgment, even the real difficulties are not fatal to my theory.

Difficulties and objections to my theory fall into four groups:

First, if species have descended from other species by a series of many small steps, why do we not see countless **transitional forms** everywhere? Why is not all nature in confusion instead of each species being well defined?

Second, is it possible that an animal with, for instance, the structure and habits of a bat could have been formed by changes to some animal with wholly different habits? Can natural selection modify existing forms to produce new structures—structures that are of trifling importance, such as the tail that a giraffe uses as a flyflapper, and also organs of wonderful structure,

Transitional, or intermediate, forms are those that show steps or stages in the transition (movement or shift) between one type of life-form and another.

Darwin's study as it looked in 1932, fifty years after his death. It was here that he wrestled with objections to his theory.

such as the eye, the perfection of which we do not yet fully understand?

Third, can instincts be acquired and modified through natural selection? How shall we explain the marvelous instinct that leads the bee to build a honeycomb out of wax cells that are mathematically advanced?

Fourth, why does the interbreeding of two species produce hybrid offspring that are sterile, while the interbreeding of two varieties within the same species produces fertile offspring?

Instinct is the subject of Chapter Seven. Interbreeding and hybrids form the subject of Chapter Eight. The first two issues—transitional forms and structures of great complexity—are discussed in this chapter.

The Lack of In-Between Forms

Natural selection and extinction go hand in hand. Each new form, improved with modifications, will tend to outcompete and finally replace its parent species, as well as the less improved transitional forms with which it competes. If we look at each species as descended from some other form, both the parent form and all the transitional varieties will generally have been exterminated by the time the species reached its present form.

By this theory, innumerable transitional forms must have existed in the past, and have become extinct. Why do we not find them embedded in countless numbers in the crust of the Earth? I will discuss this question in Chapter Nine, on fossils and the geological record.

But what about transitional forms among the species alive today? Some may say that when several closely related species live in the same area, we surely ought to find many living transitional forms between them.

Let us take a simple example. When we travel from north to south over a continent, we generally meet a series of related species, each filling nearly the same place in the economy of nature. These species often meet and intermingle in the zone between their two ranges. As we move south, the species from

"Natural selection and extinction go hand in hand."

north of the intermingling zone become rarer and rarer. The species from south of the zone become more and more common, until they have entirely replaced the northern species. But if we compare examples of these species in the zone where they intermingle, they are as distinct from one another as examples from farther north and farther south would be.

By my theory, these related northern and southern species have descended from a common parent. Each has become adapted to the conditions of its own region. But in the intermediate zone where the two regions meet, conditions of life are intermediate, too. Why do we not find closely linking intermediate varieties between the northern and the southern species?

This difficulty for a long time quite confounded me. But I think it can be in large part explained.

We generally find a species tolerably numerous over most of its range. It becomes rarer toward the edge of its range, and finally it disappears. The neutral or intermediate zone between the ranges of two related species is usually narrow compared with the range of each species.

Remember that almost every species, even where it is most numerous, would increase immensely in numbers if not for competing species. Nearly all species either prey on others, or are preyed on by them. In short, each living thing is interconnected, either directly or indirectly, with other living things.

The range of any species does not depend only on physical conditions such as climate. It also depends in large part on the presence of other species. These other species do not blend one into another by tiny, almost-invisible degrees. They are sharply defined.

The geographic range of any one species also tends to be sharply defined. And because each species exists in lower numbers on the outskirts of its range, if something happens there that harms the species—if its enemies increase, or its prey decreases, or the seasons are extreme—the species may be exterminated on the outskirts of its range. This would make its overall range still more sharply defined.

The range of a species includes all the places it occurs naturally. This map shows the range of *Ilex opaca*, the American holly.

An 1872 engraving of merino sheep in Spain.

Species that exist in small numbers are more at risk of extermination than species that exist in large numbers. Because an intermediate form would exist in smaller numbers than the closely related forms on both sides of it, it would be more liable to be wiped out on the basis of numbers alone.

But the effect of natural selection itself is far more important, I believe. My theory is that varieties are modified into distinct species. The varieties that inhabit larger areas and exist in larger numbers will have a great advantage over intermediate varieties that exist in smaller numbers in a narrow zone between those areas.

Forms of life that exist in larger numbers will always have a better chance of producing favorable variations because they have more individuals—which means more raw material for natural selection to work on. In the race for life, common and numerous forms of life will be modified and improved faster than others. They will tend to beat and replace forms that are less common and numerous.

I will show what I mean with an imaginary example of artificial selection on three breeds of domestic sheep. The first is adapted to a large mountainous region. The second is adapted to a narrow strip of hilly land. The third is adapted to the wide plains at the base of the hills.

All the sheep owners try with equal skill to improve their breeds by selection. Yet two sets of sheep owners—those on the great expanses of mountains and plains—will likely improve their breeds faster than the sheep owners on the small hilly tract in between. Why should that be the case?

The hilly region is smaller than the other two regions, which means that the number of sheep there will be smaller as well. Sheep owners in this region will have fewer variations that they can use to improve their breed. As a result, the improved mountain or plain breed will take the place of the hill breed. In the end, the mountain and plain breeds, which began with the advantage of greater numbers, will come into close contact with each other, without the hill breed between them.

Gliding Squirrels and Flying Fish

Opponents of views such as mine have asked how, for instance, a meat-eating land animal could have been turned into a water dweller. How could the animal have lived in its transitional state?

Yet it would be easy to show that within certain groups of meat-eating animals, creatures exist in a range of conditions between water and land. The American mink, for instance, has webbed feet like other swimming creatures. It resembles an otter in its fur, short legs, and tail. In summer the mink may live like an otter, diving for fish, but during the long winter it leaves the frozen waters. Then, like its relatives the polecats and weasels, it preys on mice and land animals.

An Indian giant flying squirrel, *Petaurista philippensis*, glides from one tree to another.

I have collected many striking cases of transition in the animal kingdom. Some of them show how a single species, like the mink, may have many different habits. A few of them show transitional habits and structures in closely related species.

Look at the family of squirrels. Here we have the finest gradation of body types. Some species of squirrels have their tails only slightly flattened, while others have the back part of their bodies widened, with the skin on their sides rather loose, like the beginning of a flap. Still others, the flying squirrels, have a broad flap of skin that joins their four limbs and even the base of the tail. This flap, like a parachute, allows them to glide through the air to an astonishing distance from tree to tree.

Each structure is useful to each kind of squirrel in its own country, by letting it escape birds or beasts of prey, or collect food more quickly, or survive occasional falls. But this does not mean that the structure of each squirrel is the best that it is possible to imagine under all conditions.

Suppose the climate and vegetation changed, or competing rodents or new beasts of prey entered the country, or local species changed through modification. In any of these cases, some kinds of squirrels would decrease in numbers

Flying fish probably evolved their ability to glide through the air as a way of escaping from predators.

or become exterminated, unless they also became modified to adapt to the new conditions.

Some squirrels may seem to approach flight. Other animals, however, have wings but use them for something other than flying. If loggerheaded ducks, penguins, and ostriches were extinct or unknown, who would guess that some birds might use their wings only as flappers, like the loggerheaded duck; or as fins in the water and front legs on the land, like the penguin; or as sails, like the ostrich? The structure of each of these birds suits its particular conditions of life, for each has to live by a struggle, but it is not necessarily the best possible structure under all possible conditions.

We see that flying birds and mammals exist, as do flying insects of widely diverse types. We know that **flying reptiles** once existed, although they are now extinct. What about fish? We know several species of flying fish, which do not truly fly but rather leap from the water and glide far through the air, slightly rising and turning by the aid of their fluttering fins before plunging beneath the waves.

Can we not imagine that flying fish might, over time, be modified into perfectly winged animals? If this were to happen, who would imagine that in an early state they lived in the open ocean, and used their fins only to escape being devoured by other fish?

Flying reptiles known as pterosaurs became extinct millions of years ago, leaving no descendants. They were different from dinosaurs, which were the ancestors of today's birds.

Habit and Structure

When we see a structure that is highly developed for any habit, as a bird's wings are developed for flight, we should remember that animals with early, transitional forms of that structure will seldom exist in the present day. They will have been replaced by improvement through natural selection.

Let us return to our imaginary example of the flying fish that developed to the point where it could truly fly. Would such fish develop in a wide variety of forms, to catch many kinds of prey on land and in the water? This would not be possible until their wings were so highly developed that they gave an advantage over other animals in the battle for life. The early, transitional forms—those whose fins were still developing into true wings—would be outnumbered by the greater variety of highly developed forms that appeared later. This is why fossils of species with transitional stages of a structure will always be rarer than fossils of species with fully developed structures. There will have been fewer individuals belonging to transitional species.

It sometimes happens that within a single species, individuals follow changed habits. One example is the many British insects that now feed on plants that are not native to Britain. Brought from distant places, these plants now form part of the life of insects in Britain.

Individuals of the same type may also follow different habits. In South America, I have often watched **tyrant flycatchers** hovering over one spot and then proceeding to another, as the **kestrel** does. But at other times a tyrant flycatcher will stand stationary on the edge of water, then dash like a kingfisher at a fish.

We sometimes see individuals of a species following habits widely different from those of their own species and other species in the same genus. By my theory, we might expect that such individuals would occasionally give rise to new species with unusual habits, and with their structure modified from that of their parent species. Such cases do occur in nature.

Can a more striking instance of adaptation be given than that of woodpeckers, so well suited for climbing trees and seizing insects in the chinks of the bark? Yet in North America there are woodpeckers that feed largely on fruit, and others with elongated wings that chase insects in flight. On the plains of South America, where not a tree grows, there is a woodpecker that closely resembles our common species in structure, coloring, flight, and even the harsh tone of its voice. Yet it is a woodpecker that never climbs a tree!

Tyrant flycatchers are a large and varied family of songbirds. Most, but not all, of these species eat insects.

Kestrels are small falcons.

The Andean flicker is a South American woodpecker species found in open, treeless terrain.

Anyone who believes that each being has been created as we now see it must occasionally feel surprise when seeing an animal whose habits do not match its structure. What can be plainer than that the webbed feet of ducks and geese are formed for swimming? Yet there are upland geese with webbed feet that rarely or never go near the water. The frigatebird is seen far out at sea and has all its toes webbed, yet no one except **Audubon** has seen it land on the surface of the sea. On the other hand, grebes and coots are water birds, although their toes are not webbed but only bordered by membrane. In such cases—and many others—habits and structure do not match. It is likely that habits have changed without a change in structure.

Recall that every organic being is constantly trying to increase in numbers. If any plant or animal varies even a little in its habits or structure from others of its kind, and if this variation gives it an advantage over another plant or animal, it will seize the place of that plant or animal, however different from its original place.

John James Audubon (1785–1851) was an American naturalist and artist best known today for his close study and detailed paintings of birds.

Evolution and the Eye

Eyes might seem to be a great difficulty for my theory. I freely confess that it seems absurd to suppose that natural selection could have formed the eye, with its complex mechanisms for adjusting focus to different distances, for letting in different amounts of light, and for correctly seeing color and shape.

Yet reason tells me that the difficulty is overcome if certain conditions are met. Do there exist in nature many stages between a perfect and complex eye and a very imperfect and simple eye, with each stage each being useful to its possessor? Do eyes vary ever so slightly, and are these variations inherited? Is it true that a variation or modification in the eye might be useful when the conditions of life change?

The answer to all these questions is yes. Therefore, we must believe that natural selection, working slowly, modifying the structure of the simple eye by preserving useful variations, could produce the complex eye.

"Just a Theory"?

You may have brushed something aside by saying, "It's just a theory." If so, you probably used "theory" to mean something like "idea" or "possibility" or even "guess." When people dismiss something as a theory, they usually mean that it isn't a fact.

"Theory" is used in many ways, but in science it has several precise meanings.

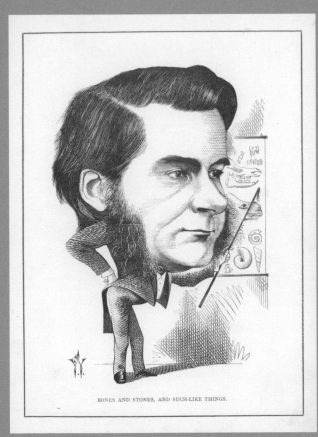

BONES AND STONES, AND SUCH-LIKE THINGS.

A theory can be the set of basic principles, or foundation, of a body of knowledge. People study music theory and game theory, for example, because these are bodies of knowledge that rest on basic principles.

Scientists also use "theory" to mean "a convincing or scientifically acceptable explanation for things that have been observed." An example is the modern theory of light, which says that light sometimes behaves like a wave and at other times like a particle. This theory explains everything known about the behavior of light; it accurately predicts how light will behave; and it has been tested and supported by many experiments.

That is how Darwin used "theory."

Time and time again in the *Origin*, Darwin speaks of "my theory." His theory was "descent with modification" (now called "evolution") by means of natural selection. It said nothing about the origin of life. Instead, Darwin's theory was about the pattern of change in living things over the history of the Earth, and the way new species arise. Darwin believed his theory was the best explanation for the many, many facts he and other naturalists had

A caricature of biologist Thomas Henry Huxley. He was called "Darwin's bulldog" for his strong defense of Darwin's theory of evolution by natural selection.

gathered: facts about domestic and wild animals and plants, about species living and extinct, and about the differences and similarities among various forms of life. Darwin's theory has been tested and accepted by the scientific community, and now it is a key part of biological science.

Evolution is both a theory and a fact. It has been observed in action. That doesn't mean that it is fully understood. Scientists are still studying natural selection and the other mechanisms of evolution. They are still learning about the blueprints of life and how they change over time. New discoveries will surely change and enlarge our understanding of evolution. That's how science works—theories change and adapt when new information comes to light.

Darwin was wrong about some details of his theory. He underestimated the age of the Earth, for example. And where extinction was concerned, some modern experts think Darwin gave too much weight to competition among species and not enough to factors such as climate change. He made little mistakes, too, such as claiming that the modern chicken had descended from the wrong species of junglefowl. Still, Darwin was right about the big picture. Species come from other species, in a chain of life that links all organic beings together.

Arthropods are animals that lack spines, have skeletons in the form of shells on the outsides of their bodies, and have legs with joints that bend. The arachnids are spiders and their relatives. The crustaceans are crabs and their relatives.

Some caterpillars have this type of eye. When they change into adult insects, they will have more complex eyes, with lenses. Certain non-arthropods, such as flatworms and jellyfish, also have simple eyes like these.

In looking for the stages of development of any organ in any species, we should look at that species' ancestors—but this is scarcely ever possible, because many parent species are extinct. We are forced to look instead at related species, those that have descended from the same parent form. In them we may see what stages are possible, and whether any have come down through time without much change from earlier forms.

We find many stages of development of the eye in the living species of arthropods. This large phylum includes insects, arachnids, and crustaceans. Some dwell on land, some in water. Some fly, some spend most of their lives underground.

The simplest arthropod eye is an optic nerve coated with pigment, without any other mechanism. From this basic stage, numerous gradations of structure exist, until we reach a moderately complex eye. Certain crustaceans, for instance, have a double cornea. The inner one is divided into flat sections; inside each section is a lens-shaped swelling. In other crustacean eyes, transparent cones coated with pigment are shaped so that the light that enters them must converge, or be focused, on a point.

These facts show that there are many stages of diversity in the eyes of living arthropods. I can see no very great difficulty in believing that natural selection has turned the simple optic nerve coated with pigment into a variety of other, more complex forms.

A reader who finds, after finishing this book, that many facts otherwise unexplainable can be explained by the theory of descent should admit that even the perfect eye of an eagle might be formed by natural selection, although the transitional grades are unknown.

If it could be demonstrated that any complex organ exists that cannot

A female mantis shrimp with its eye on a stalk. While human eyes have three types of light-detecting structures (to see red, green, and blue), mantis shrimp have between twelve and fourteen types of such structures, some of which detect ultraviolet light.

possibly have been formed by a series of many slight modifications, my theory would absolutely break down. But I can find no such case.

Electric Eels and Fireflies

What of cases in which the same organ appears in species that are not at all closely related? Can these also be the result of natural selection?

The electric organs of fish present a difficulty. If electric organs had been inherited from a single ancient ancestor, we might expect all electric fishes to be closely related to one another, but they are not. Electric organs occur in only about a dozen species, and several of these species belong to very remotely related groups. Nor is there any fossil evidence to suggest that in the past most fishes had electric organs, now lost by most of their descendants.

A similar case is the luminous or light-producing organs in a few insects, such as fireflies. The luminous insects are found in various families and orders. How is it that the same kind of organ has formed in all of them?

In these cases of very different species with what seems to be the same organ, it is important to note that although the organ may look and act the same, there is still generally some difference in it from species to species. In the same way that two people have sometimes independently hit on the very same invention, I believe that natural selection, working for the good of each being and taking advantage of different variations, has sometimes produced the same results in organic beings that are only distantly related.

Hard as it may be to imagine how an organ reached its present state, I have been astonished how rarely an organ can be named that has no transitional stage leading toward it. The truth of this is shown by an old saying in natural history: *Natura non facit saltum*, meaning "Nature makes no leap." On the theory of natural selection, we can clearly understand why this is so. Natural selection can act only by taking advantage of slight variations, with each variation building upon those that came before. Nature can never take a leap, but must advance by the shortest and slowest steps.

Some species of fish, such as electric eels, have organs that can produce electricity. They use the electricity either to stun their prey or to help them navigate and communicate with other fish.

Biologists now use the term "convergent evolution" for this observation of Darwin's. Convergent evolution means that different groups of living things have separately evolved the same feature or structure with the same function, such as the wings of bats, birds, and insects.

CHAPTER SEVEN

Instinct

An instinct as wonderful as that of the honeybee making its six-sided cells inside a honeycomb may seem hard to explain. Let us see if it is hard enough to overthrow my whole theory.

An action that we ourselves would need experience or training to perform is usually said to be instinctive when it is done by an animal. This is especially true if the animal is very young, with no experience, and also when many individual animals do the same thing in the same way.

In instincts, one action follows another by a sort of rhythm. We see this in our own species at times. If you interrupt someone who is singing a song or repeating anything learned by memory, that person may have to go back and start again to recover the train of thought.

One researcher found the same thing in a caterpillar that makes a very complicated cocoon out of silk threads. The researcher took a caterpillar that had completed its hammock up to the sixth stage of construction, and put it into a hammock that was complete only to the third stage. The caterpillar simply

Arctic terns make the longest migration on the planet—as much as 59,650 miles (95,997 kilometers)—as they fly from the Arctic to the Antarctic and back each year.

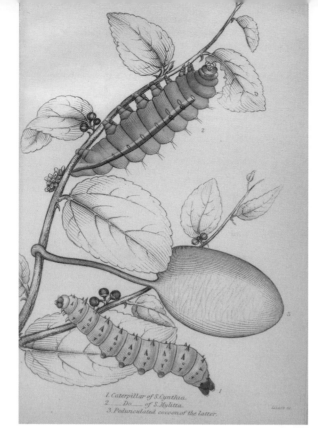

Caterpillars building a cocoon, from a book
published in 1843.

1. Caterpillar of S. Cynthia.
2. __ Do. __ of S. Mylitta.
3. Pedunculated cocoon of the latter.

Darwin was correct that instinctive behavior is inherited. Scientists today define "instinct" as a pattern of behavior seen across a species, not learned or based on the experiences of individuals. Like physical form, instinct is genetic and has occasional variations. Also like physical form, instinct can be influenced by environment and the conditions of an individual's life.

repeated the fourth, fifth, and sixth stages of construction. But when a caterpillar was taken out of a hammock made to the third stage, and placed in a hammock finished to the sixth stage, the caterpillar did not benefit from the work that was already done for it. To complete its hammock, it seemed forced to start from the third stage, where it had left off.

Instincts are as important as physical structures for the welfare of each species. They help an insect or animal survive in its conditions of life. Under changed conditions, then, slight modifications of instinct might be helpful. If it can be shown that instincts do vary even a little, I can see no reason why natural selection would not preserve and build up any variations that are good for the organism.

This is how I believe all the most complex and wonderful instincts have originated. They have been produced by natural selection acting on accidental variations of instincts. Those variations come from the same unknown causes that produce slight variations in physical form.

Instinct and Natural Selection

No complex instinct can be produced through natural selection except by the slow and gradual building up of many small, but helpful, variations. I have been surprised to find how often we can discover steps leading to the most complex instincts.

Two things are needed for natural selection to act on instinct. One is some variation in an organism's instincts. The other is the passing of such variation to the organism's offspring.

Instincts certainly do vary. One example is the migratory instinct of birds. Within the same species, some birds travel different distances and directions than others, and some seem to have lost the instinct to migrate. The same thing is true of nest building by birds. Nests of birds in a single species vary partly because of the locations on which they are built, such as branches or roofs, and partly on the temperature and the building materials that are available where the birds live. But nest building often varies from causes wholly unknown to us.

Another example of instinct that varies is animals' fear of humans. Species that live on deserted islands and have had no contact with humans are not at first fearful of people, but they slowly gain instinctive fear. Even in England we see that our large birds are more fearful than our small birds, because the large birds have been most hunted and killed by humans. On uninhabited islands, large birds are no more fearful than small ones.

To understand how natural selection has shaped instincts in a state of nature, let us consider two examples. First is the instinct that leads a bird to lay her eggs in other birds' nests. Second is the honeycomb-making power of the honeybee—generally ranked by naturalists as one of the most wonderful of all known instincts.

The Curious Case of the Cuckoo's Eggs

The cuckoo is known to lay its eggs in the nests of other species. What strange instinct would cause a mother bird to abandon her eggs to be hatched and raised by others?

It is generally believed that the cause of this instinct is that the cuckoo lays her eggs not one a day, but one every two or three days. If she built her own nest and sat on her own eggs, there would be eggs and young birds of different ages in the same nest, and the process of laying and hatching might be inconveniently long, especially as cuckoos migrate early. But how did the instinct come about?

Let us suppose that the ancient ancestor of our European cuckoo made her own nest and had both eggs and young birds in the nest at the same time—but that once in a while she laid an egg in another bird's nest. If the mother bird profited by this occasional habit, or if her offspring were stronger

Darwin was writing about the European cuckoo, one of several bird species that are nest parasites, which means that they lay their eggs in the nests of other species. The parent birds of the other species raise the nest parasites' hatchlings, which often kill the parents' own young.

Reed warblers feed a hungry young cuckoo that has taken the place of their own young.

because they were taken care of by another bird, then either the mother bird or the young raised elsewhere would gain an advantage.

I am led to believe that these young would inherit their mother's occasional and unusual habit. They in turn would be likely to lay eggs in other birds' nests, and this would make them successful in producing offspring. As the process continued, I believe that the strange instinct of the cuckoo could be—and has been—created.

Bees as Builders

Only a dull observer can examine the exquisite structure of a honeycomb, so beautifully adapted to its purpose, without enthusiastic admiration.

Mathematicians tell us that bees make their cells of just the right shape to hold the greatest possible amount of honey while using the smallest possible amount of precious wax to build them. It has been said that a skillful worker with tools and measures would find it very difficult to make wax cells like those of the bees, although a crowd of bees working in a dark hive can do it perfectly. How can they make all the necessary angles and surfaces, or tell when they are correctly made?

The difficulty is not nearly so great as it at first appears. All this beautiful work can be shown, I think, to follow from a few very simple instincts.

Let us look to the great principle of gradation, or small steps along the way, and see whether Nature reveals to us her method of work. The comb-building styles of three different kinds of bees range from crude and lumpy to elegant and mathematically perfect. We can imagine changes in instinct, leading to small changes in comb building, that would lead from the crudest building style to the most elegant.

The crudest structures are made by species of bumblebees that use their old cocoons to hold honey. Sometimes these bees add short tubes of wax to the mouths of the cocoons to make them longer. They also use wax to make separate and very irregular rounded cells.

The most elegant structures are made by the honeybees that create honeycombs to hold honey or young bees. The combs are made out of wax. They consist of many separate compartments called cells. The cells are nested together, side to side and back to back, in a double layer.

A honeycomb holds bee larvae in various stages of growth.

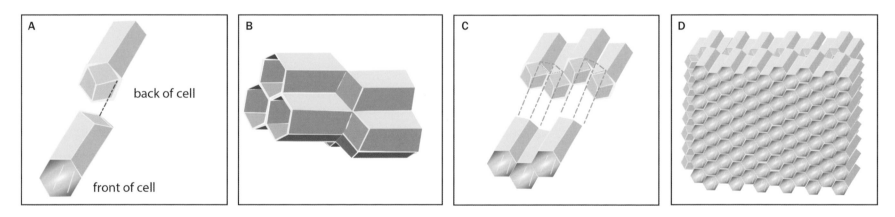

A   back of cell   front of cell

B

C

D

Darwin admired the "elegant structures" that honeybees make by instinct. The basic unit of these structures is the cell, a tube with six flat sides. The front is open. The back is made of three triangular plates that rise up from the ends of the six sides to form a pyramid.

Cells are joined together back-to-back. The three plates of the pyramid at the back of each cell also form part of the backs of three other cells. (A) The plate highlighted blue is the same surface in two different cells.

Cells are formed in clusters, with their open front ends pointing in opposite directions. (B) As they are built up, each cell shares its side walls with six other cells pointing in the same direction. It shares its back wall with three cells pointing in the opposite direction. (C) Together, the double stack of cells forms a honeycomb. (D)

Each honeybee cell is open on the front. All of them tilt slightly upward, which keeps the contents from falling out. Each cell is a six-sided chamber. Its back and side walls also serve as walls for the cells behind it and next to it. The rear of each cell is made up of three plates of wax that form an outward-pointing pyramid, which locks into place between the outward-pointing pyramids on the backs of the cells behind it. All the cells are fitted together in this way.

Between the bumblebee's crude, lumpy combs and the honeybee's elegant honeycombs, we have the cells of the Mexican bee. This bee has a physical structure between that of the bumblebee and the honeybee, but closer to the bumblebee. It builds a wax comb of nearly identical tube-shaped cells in which the young are hatched.

The Mexican bee also builds a different, larger kind of cell to hold honey. These honey cells are in the shape of hollow balls clumped into an irregular mass. The important point is that these cells are so close to one another that they would break into one another if the balls were made perfectly round. But the bees never do this. Instead, they build flat walls of wax between balls that would otherwise join one another.

Each of the Mexican bee's honey cells therefore is made up of an outer globelike part and two, three, or more flat surfaces, depending on whether the cell joins two, three, or more other cells. When one cell comes into contact with three other cells, the flat surfaces form a pyramid, like a rough version of the pyramid-shaped rear walls of honeybee cells.

If the Mexican bee made its honey cells always at the same distance from one another, and all the same size, and arranged them in a double layer, the result would probably look like the comb of the honeybee, but shorter from front to back. If the Mexican bee then made its cells longer by adding tubes of wax to them, as the bumblebee does, its comb would be even more like the honeybee's.

In other words, if we could slightly modify the instincts of the Mexican bee, this bee would make a structure as wonderful as that of the honeybee. I believe that the honeybee has gained her unique architectural powers through modifications to the simple instincts we see in other bee species.

Instinct and Inheritance

I have tried in this chapter to show that instincts vary slightly in a state of nature. No one will deny that instincts are of the highest importance to each animal. I see no difficulty in natural selection building up slight modifications of instinct in any way that is useful to an animal.

Instincts are not always absolutely perfect. They are liable to mistakes. The migrating instinct of a bird may fail, causing the bird to end up hundreds of miles off course. Even the honeybee occasionally makes a misshapen cell or an irregular comb.

A few other facts about instincts strengthen the argument for natural selection. Take the case of species that are closely related yet live in widely separate parts of the world, under different conditions. Such species often have nearly the same instincts, because they have inherited them from shared ancestors.

Inheritance explains why the thrush of South America lines its nest with mud, in the same manner as our British thrush.

It also explains why the male wrens of both North America and Britain, although they are of different species, build similar nests to roost in while they are wooing females—a **habit wholly unlike** that of any other known bird.

We may feel that certain instincts are cruel. Young cuckoos hatch from eggs left in the nests of other species, then often throw the baby birds of those species out of their nests. Ants make slaves of other ants. Wasps lay their eggs in live caterpillars, which are then eaten from inside by the wasp larvae. To my imagination it is far more satisfactory to see such instincts not as specially created, but as the results of a law that applies to all organic beings: multiply, vary, let the strongest live and the weakest die.

A thrush's nest. Mud, carried to the nest in the birds' beaks, coats the inside of the nest to make it smooth and solid.

Working on their own, male wrens build up to a dozen nests during mating season, hoping to attract a female. Darwin rightly saw this as a sign that North American and British wrens share an ancestor, but he was wrong about one thing: males of some other bird species do build nests alone, although more often males and females build them together.

CHAPTER EIGHT

Rules and Mules

In the vast majority of cases, when two species are artificially **crossed**, the result is sterility. Either the two species fail to produce offspring when they are crossed, or the cross does produce **hybrid** offspring, but those hybrids are sterile, unable to produce offspring of their own.

Most naturalists believe that species were created just as they exist now, and that they were created with the quality of sterility to prevent interbreeding, which would blend all organic forms into confusion. But if we suppose that species came into being as a result of natural selection, sterility raises an important question. The sterility of hybrids could not possibly be of any advantage to them. How, then, could natural selection have given species a quality that prevents them from interbreeding to produce fertile offspring?

Crosses are the interbreeding of two species or two varieties.

Hybrids are the offspring produced by crosses.

A mule train in the Grand Canyon. People have long crossbred horses and donkeys to obtain mules, which are valued as load carriers because they are sturdy and sure-footed.

Many mythological creatures are imaginary hybrids, or blends of different species. In a scene from Greek myth, the warrior Bellerophon rides his horse, Pegasus, which has the wings of a bird, into battle with the Chimera, a mixture of lion, goat, and serpent.

I hope to show that sterility is not a specially created quality. It is a byproduct of other differences gained through natural processes.

Fertility and Sterility

Fertility and sterility apply differently to species than they do to varieties. When plants or animals of one species are crossed with another species, they generally produce no offspring, or only a few. This is true in the vast majority of cases, even if the individual plants or animals have already produced offspring with partners of their own species.

When crosses of two species *do* produce hybrid offspring, such as the **mule** or **hinny** that results from the mating of a horse and a donkey, the hybrids themselves are generally unable to produce offspring, due to some imperfection in their reproductive systems. The end result of the cross is sterility, because even when it produces offspring, the offspring cannot reproduce.

Now consider varieties, or different forms within a single species. When varieties are crossed, they are generally fertile. That means that not only do these crosses produce offspring, but the offspring are also able to reproduce.

This difference in fertility and sterility seems to show that varieties and species are quite distinct: varieties can be crossed, while species cannot be crossed. But let us take a closer look at a few cases of crosses between species. We will see that sterility and fertility are not always absolute. There can be degrees of each.

A mule is the hybrid offspring of a female horse and a male donkey. A hinny is the hybrid offspring of a male horse and a female donkey.

Crossing Two Plant Species

Plants of various species show different degrees of sterility when crossed. When crosses between related species do produce hybrid offspring, fertility does not always disappear completely among these offspring. It may fade away in stages over generations.

Yet many observers suggest that sterility is highly common in crosses between plant species. One expert said that *all* crosses between plant species are sterile. However, when he found that two forms thought by most experts to be separate species were quite fertile when crossed together, he unhesitatingly declared them to be varieties, not species.

Another expert who claims that crosses between plant species result in sterility bases his argument on numbers. He carefully counts the seeds—if any—

Reproductive Isolation

Throughout the *Origin*, Darwin argued against the traditional view that species were fixed and unchanging. He had realized that not only are species mutable, or changeable, but that a species can change so much that in time it becomes a whole new species.

This chapter is part of that argument. In it, Darwin argues against what nearly everyone in his time believed: that species were specially created in their present form. People believed that different species could never, or almost never, crossbreed, because interbreeding between the species would cause a chaotic blending. The purpose of sterility was to be a sturdy barrier against such chaos.

In examining fertility and sterility when species interbreed (and also in the hybrid offspring produced by some of these crosses), Darwin wanted to show that the barrier

between species is not completely solid but has a few weak spots. He pointed out that while fertile crosses between species and fertile hybrids are rare, they do occur once in a while. This supported Darwin's claim that fertility and sterility are not fixed and absolute. Instead they have a natural variation, like other traits possessed by plants and animals.

Darwin defined "species" more loosely than modern biologists do. (See "Lumpers and Splitters" in Chapter Two for more about the modern approach to identifying species.) To Darwin, the categories "species" and "variety" blended together, and a species did not have hard-and-fast boundaries. But to a modern scientist, species that reproduce sexually—by blending the reproductive cells of two parents—are defined by reproductive isolation. (Species are harder to define in bacteria and other organisms that do not reproduce sexually.)

"Reproductive isolation" does not refer to a lonely animal that can't find a mate, or a solitary plant with no source of fertilizing pollen nearby. It refers to all the factors that prevent one species from interbreeding with another to produce fertile offspring. Those factors can be genetic—something in the DNA of the two species that prevents fertilization from occurring when they mate, or prevents

offspring from developing normally. But reproductive isolation can also come from geographic factors (the species breed in different places) or behavioral ones (the species do not seek one another out for mating). This is why species that do not interbreed in the wild occasionally do so in unnatural environments such as zoos.

If individuals from two species *do* produce fertile offspring, scientists reconsider whether the parents really belong to separate species. For example, fertile pups can be born from crosses among coyotes, wolves, and dogs, which leads some biologists to claim that all three are subspecies of a single species.

Another difference between Darwin and modern biologists is that scientists now understand the genetic basis for sterility. Darwin knew that horses and donkeys can cross to produce mules and hinnies, and that these hybrids are sterile, but he did not know why. We now know that it is because horses and donkeys have different numbers of chromosomes Their genetic material can combine to create offspring, but it does not equip those offspring with functioning reproductive cells.

There have, however, been a very few cases of female mules and hinnies producing offspring when mated with male horses or donkeys. Scientists think this rare event may happen when the female's chromosomes just happen to line up to those of the male. Darwin would point to these rarities as proof that the barriers between species give way once in a while, and that sterility is not an argument against his theory.

Three young coywolves, the offspring of artificial breeding between a male western gray wolf and a female western coyote, are part of a research project to determine whether wolves and coyotes interbreed in the wild.

that are produced when two species are artificially crossed. He then counts the seeds that their hybrid offspring produce. Next, he compares these figures with the number of seeds that the two parent species produce in nature, when bred with their own species. The hybrids produce fewer seeds than the pure parent species, which this expert sees as evidence of some degree of sterility.

I see a serious cause of error in this argument. Nearly all the plants that this researcher experimented on were kept in pots in his house. Such conditions often make a plant less fertile. We may doubt whether many other species are really as sterile when crossed as he believes.

On the other hand, the fertility of pure species is easily affected by circumstances such as changes in temperature or rainfall, or the lack of insects to pollinate blooms.

For all practical purposes, it is hard to say where fertility ends and sterility begins in plants. The best evidence of this is that the two experts already mentioned came to different conclusions about the very same species.

Some plants, such as certain species of **lobelia**, can be far more easily fertilized by the pollen of another species than by their own—even when their own pollen was found to be perfectly good, for it fertilized another distinct species. This means that certain plants can actually be hybridized much more readily than they can be self-fertilized!

We know that fertility and sterility vary among individuals of the same species. Some individuals produce many offspring. Others produce fewer offspring, or none at all. In the same way, individuals of a species seem to vary in how fertile they may be when crossed with another species.

Lobelias in bloom.

Lobelias are a genus of flowering plants with more than four hundred known species.

Crossing Two Animal Species

Experiments in crossing animal species have been far fewer than those with plants. It is especially difficult to carry out experiments on animals that do not breed freely in captivity. For instance, the domesticated canary bird, a type of

A muntjac, a small Asian deer, in a forest in Nepal.

finch, has been crossed with nine other finch species, but not one of those finch species is easy to breed in captivity. This may be one reason why neither their crosses nor their hybrids are perfectly fertile.

I do not know of any thoroughly authenticated cases of fertile hybrid animals. I do, however, have some reason to believe that fertile hybrids have been produced from crosses between two species of muntjac. The same is said to be true of crosses between various species of pheasants.

Looking at these facts on the interbreeding of plant and animal species, most crosses and hybrids show some degree of sterility—but sterility cannot, in our present state of knowledge, be considered absolutely universal.

Rules of Reproduction

We will now consider the circumstances and rules governing the sterility of crosses between species and of hybrids. Do these rules show that species have specially been given this sterility to prevent their crossing and blending together in utter confusion?

The following rules and conclusions are chiefly drawn from studies on plants by some of our leading botanists. I have taken pains to see how far the rules apply to animals. Considering our scanty knowledge of hybrid animals, I have been surprised to find that the same rules generally apply to both kingdoms.

I have already pointed out that fertility, both of crosses between species and of the hybrid offspring of crossed species, exists in many degrees, from zero to complete fertility. The absolute zero of fertility is seen when pollen from a plant of one **family** is placed on the reproductive organ of a plant in a different family. It has no more effect than so much dust.

But consider what happens when species within the same genus are crossed. Suppose that plants of species A receive pollen from species B, C, D, and E in their genus, with each individual A plant receiving pollen from one of the other species. The result is that the A plants will produce different numbers of seeds along the fertility scale, up to complete fertility. In certain abnormal cases, the result is more seeds than even the plant's own pollen will produce.

From these results we can conclude that sterility and fertility occur in degrees when species are crossed.

It is the same with hybrid plants. Some hybrid plants never produce seeds,

Darwin here uses "family" as a term of biological classification: a group of related genera.

Many modern food plants are hybrid species that have been artificially created. These bitter oranges are hybrids of the mandarin orange and the pomelo.

but other hybrids fertilize themselves and produce greater and greater numbers of seeds, up to complete fertility.

Hybrids from two species that are very difficult to cross and rarely produce any offspring are generally sterile. But it is not the case that the difficulty or ease of crossing the parents is the same as the sterility or fertility of their hybrid offspring.

There are many cases in which two pure species can be easily crossed to produce numerous hybrid offspring, yet these hybrids are remarkably sterile. On the other hand, there are species that can be crossed very rarely, or with extreme difficulty, but the hybrids, when at last produced, are very fertile. Even within the same genus of plants these two opposite cases can occur.

The degree of fertility is variable, like other features of individual organisms. Fertility is not always the same even when the same two species are crossed under the same circumstances. It depends in part upon the traits of the individuals chosen for the experiment. The same is true of hybrids.

No one has been able to point out what kind of difference, or how much difference, is enough to prevent two species from being crossed to produce offspring. Plants that are widely different in habit and appearance, with strongly marked differences in every part of the flower, pollen, and fruit, can be crossed. Plants that live in different habitats and extremely different climates, even **deciduous** and evergreen trees, can often be crossed with ease. We may conclude that there is no outward clue to whether a successful cross will be possible.

Reciprocal crosses have their own rules. A reciprocal cross involves two pairings. For example, a male of one species, such as a horse, is crossed with a female of another species, such as a donkey, and a female of the first species (horse) is crossed with a male of the second species (donkey). Once a pairing has taken place in each direction, the two species are said to be reciprocally crossed.

Deciduous trees are those that, unlike evergreens, shed all their leaves at the same time each year.

The two pairings in a reciprocal cross often produce **very different results**. This difference in reciprocal crosses between the same two species has long been observed. One botanist experimented with species in the genus *Mirabilis*, called four o'clock flowers. He found that the species *M. jalapa* can easily be fertilized by the pollen of *M. longiflora* to produce fertile hybrids. But when he tried more than two hundred times, over eight years, to fertilize *M. longiflora* with the pollen of *M. jalapa*, he utterly failed.

Such cases are highly important. They prove that the ability of any two species to cross is connected with differences we cannot see, having to do with the reproductive systems. Most important for my theory, these rules and facts show that the sterility of crosses and hybrids is **not absolute**.

In reciprocal crosses of horses and donkeys, the offspring of a male horse and a female donkey is a hinny, which may be either male or female. The offspring of a female horse and a male donkey is a mule, and it also may be either male or female. Hinnies and mules differ in several ways, although both are sterile. Hinnies are produced far less often than mules. They are generally smaller than mules, with shorter ears and longer manes and tails.

Darwin is arguing that because sterility is not a complete barrier to the mixing of species, it cannot have been specially created to keep them from changing. The fact that such crosses are *generally* sterile is not enough to overthrow natural selection.

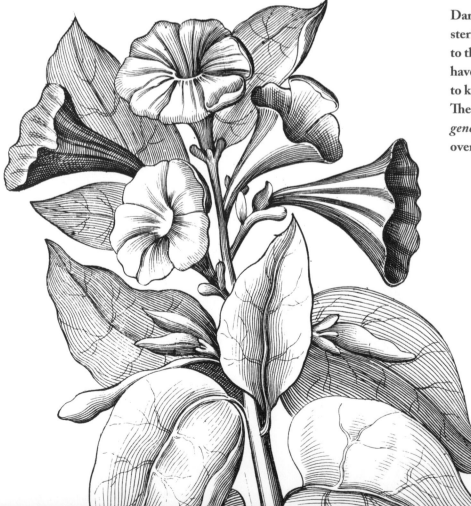

CHAPTER NINE

Reading the Rocks

In Chapter Six I listed the chief objections that might be raised against the views in this book. Most of them have now been discussed. One very obvious remaining difficulty has to do with the fossils found in the Earth's crust.

Species are distinct, meaning that they are not blended together by countless forms showing every link of the change from one species to another. In Chapter Six I gave reasons why such links do not commonly occur at the present day. I tried also to show why the intermediate varieties that connect older forms to newer ones will exist in smaller numbers than the forms they connect. The intermediate varieties will generally be beaten out and exterminated during the course of change.

Through the very process of natural selection, new varieties continually replace their parent forms and exterminate them. But because

Life-size models of extinct animals became a popular sensation in 1850s London. These two iguanodons and other Crystal Palace dinosaurs, as they are called, remain on display in Bromley, a borough of London.

this extermination has acted on an enormous scale, the number of intermediate varieties that formerly existed must be truly enormous. Why then is not every part of the Earth full of the fossil remains of intermediate links?

Geology does not reveal any such finely graduated chain of life. This is perhaps the gravest objection to my theory. The explanation lies, I believe, in the extreme imperfection of the geological record.

Where Are the In-Between Fossils?

What sort of intermediate forms must once have existed? I have found it difficult, when looking at any two species, to avoid picturing forms directly intermediate between them. But this is a wholly false view. We should look for forms that existed between those species and an unknown species that was the ancestor of both of them. This unknown ancestor will generally have been different from all its descendants.

If we look at very distinct living species, such as the horse and the tapir, we have no reason to suppose that links ever existed directly between them. Yet we know from studies of their anatomy, or structure, that the horse and tapir are more closely related to each other than either is to a deer or a cow.

Horse and tapir both descended from the same unknown parent species. This ancestor will have resembled the tapir and the horse, but its structure may have differed considerably from both—perhaps even more than the horse and tapir differ from each other.

My theory does allow for the possibility that a living form might have descended from another still-living form. In such a case, direct intermediate links will have existed between them. For this to happen, though, one form would have to remain unchanged for a very long period, while its descendants underwent great change. The principle of competition makes this a very rare event. New forms of life, being modified and better suited to the conditions around them, tend to replace the old forms.

"Why then is not every part of the Earth full of the fossil remains of intermediate links?"

An **1882** engraving of a mother tapir and her young.

By the theory of natural selection, all living species have been connected with the parent species of their genus. Those parent species, most of which are now extinct, were connected with more ancient species, and so on backward to the ancestor of each great class of living things.

The number of intermediate and transitional links between all living and extinct species must have been unthinkably great. But if my theory is true, such have lived upon this Earth.

Two polar bears (white) and four brown bears. Scientists think that *Ursus maritimus*, the polar bear, evolved from *U. arctos*, the brown bear. Because this happened recently in evolutionary time, the two species occasionally interbreed and can produce fertile hybrids.

We have not found fossil remains of such infinitely numerous connecting links. Some may say there has not been enough time for so much change to happen very slowly through natural selection. Yet geology tells us that the amount of time that has passed is so great that we can only feebly grasp it.

The Past Is Vast

Anyone who can read Sir Charles Lyell's grand work *Principles of Geology*, yet not admit how incomprehensibly vast the past periods of time have been, may at once close this volume. Reading about geology, however, is not enough to grasp the age of the Earth. A person must for years examine great piles of strata stacked on top of one another, and watch the sea at work grinding down old rocks and making fresh sediment, before hoping to grasp anything of the lapse of time.

Geologist Charles Lyell was both a scientific influence on Darwin and a friend. Lyell's account of Earth's long history was a foundation for Darwin's theory, which Lyell encouraged him to publish.

It is good to wander along lines of seacoast, when formed of moderately hard rocks, and see how the rock is broken down. The tides in most cases reach the cliffs only for a short time twice a day, and only when the waves are loaded with sand or pebbles do they eat into the cliffs. Still, in time, the base of the cliff is undermined. Huge fragments fall down. These are worn away until they can be rolled about by the waves, and then ground into pebbles, sand, or mud. But we often see boulders along the bases of cliffs, thickly clothed by seaweed. This shows how slowly they are worn away and how seldom they are rolled about!

Look at beds of sedimentary rock, many thousand feet in thickness, made of worn and rounded pebbles, each of which bears the stamp of time. How slowly must this mass have built up on the floors of ancient seas and lakes. And once those floors later rose above the waves, how gradually was that sediment eroded by wind, rain, and rivers.

One estimate of the maximum thickness of sediment layers in Great Britain adds up to 72,584 feet, nearly thirteen and three-quarters miles. Some of these layers are thin in Britain, but on the continent of Europe those same layers are thousands of feet thick. Moreover, most geologists think that enormously long periods of time passed between one layer being deposited and the next. The lofty pile of sedimentary rocks in Britain gives only a poor idea of the time that passed while they were building up. Yet what time this must have consumed!

The best evidence of passing time is the amount of erosion that the Earth has suffered in many places. I was much struck with this when viewing volcanic

Geologists in Darwin's time knew that parts of the Earth's surface had risen (called "uplift") and fallen (called "subsidence") in the distant past, changing seabeds to mountains or dry land to sea. They did not yet know that these changes are driven by the slow movement of molten rock beneath the Earth's crust. See "Drifting Continents" in Chapter Eleven for more details.

The distinct layers of the Earth's crust sometimes extend over large distances. Geologists recognize a layer by the materials it is made of and by its position above and below other known layers.

islands, which have been worn by the waves and pared all round into steep cliffs one or two thousand feet high.

The same story is even more plainly told by faults, great cracks in the Earth's surface along which the strata were heaved up on one side, or thrown down on the other. In the long ages since the Earth's crust cracked at these faults, the surface of the land has been so completely worn down that no trace of these vast dislocations is visible except in **the record of the rocks** below the surface of the land.

I am tempted to give one other case: the Weald, a wooded low-lying area between chalk cliffs in southern England. The erosion of the Weald has been a mere trifle next to the erosion of masses of strata ten thousand feet thick. Yet it is an admirable lesson to stand on the cliffs on one side of the Weald and look across at the distant cliffs on the other side. One can picture the great dome of rocks which once covered up the Weald. The slow, gradual erosion of that mass of rock by the sea must have taken at least **three hundred million years—** probably far longer.

During each of those years, over the whole world, hosts of living forms have inhabited the land and the water. What an infinite number of generations, which the mind cannot grasp, must have followed one another in the long roll of years! Now turn to our richest geological museums, and what a paltry display we behold!

The Limits of Our Fossil Collections

Our paleontological collections are very imperfect. Many of our fossil species are known from a single specimen, often broken, or from just a few specimens found in one place. Only a small portion of the Earth's surface has been geologically explored. Many fossil finds remain to be discovered, as proven by the important discoveries made every year in Europe.

No living thing that is entirely soft can be preserved. Even hard parts such

Faults can be seen as vertical divides in canyon walls or cliffs; the horizontal rock layers on one side of the divide are higher than the same layers on the other side, showing that one side rose or fell long ago, although the surface at the top of the cliff or wall has been worn smooth.

Modern geologists have found the Weald to be younger than Darwin thought. The rock layers of the Weald started forming about 140 million years ago. Erosion started around sixty-five million years ago.

as shells and bones will decay and disappear, if there is no sediment to build up over them and preserve them. And even remains that do become embedded in beds of sand or gravel may be dissolved by rainwater flowing through the beds.

Sedimentary rock on Crete. The layers formed through the slow buildup of sediment during periods when the land was a flat seabed. Earth movements then bent them into folds and faults.

By "land shells" Darwin meant land-dwelling snails, members of the mollusk phylum. In 1852 geologist Charles Lyell had discovered fossils of land mollusks in Nova Scotia.

Earth and life are now known to be older than even the most revolutionary nineteenth-century scientists thought. Geological time is measured in thousands of millions (billions) of years that fall into six major eras, each of which is divided into periods, which are then divided into epochs. The present moment in Earth's history is the Holocene epoch of the Quaternary period of the Cenozoic era.

With respect to the plants and animals that lived on land in the Paleozoic and Mesozoic eras, our evidence from fossil remains is extremely limited. For instance, no land shells are known from either of these vast periods, with **one North American exception**. In regard to fossils of mammals, their preservation is accidental and rare.

But the main cause of imperfection in the geological record is that fossil-bearing layers are separated from one another by wide intervals of time. When we see these layers of formations listed in books, or when we follow them in nature, it is easy to think they closely followed one another. But we know from geological research that fossil-bearing formations do not form at a steady rate. They form at intervals, taking shape at different times in different parts of the world.

In places such as Russia and North America, wide gaps of time often passed between the formation of one fossil-bearing layer and the next. If the most skillful geologist examined only these large territories, he would never

Geochronological scale (millions of years ago)

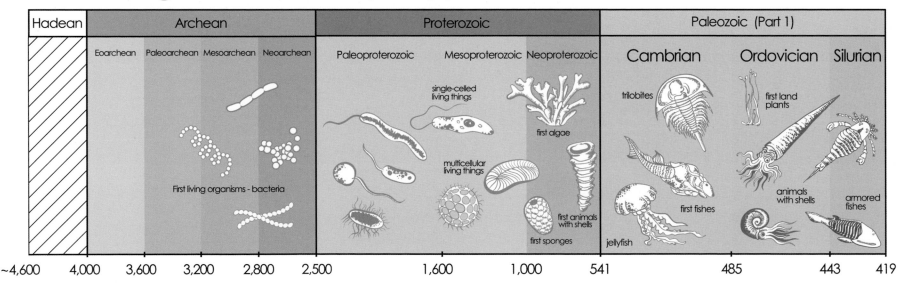

suspect that during their blank and barren periods, great piles of sediment, filled with new and peculiar forms of life, had built up in other parts of the world.

We can see why the geological formations of each region have not followed one another closely. When I examined many hundred miles of the South American coasts, I saw no recent sediment layers that would last for even a short geological period. As soon as deposits along the coast are brought up by the slow and gradual rising of the land, they are worn away by the grinding action of the waves. Along the whole west coast, probably no record of today's marine life will be preserved to the distant future.

Sediment must build up in great masses to withstand the ceaseless action of the waves upon it, first when the land is upraised and later if it sinks and rises again. Such thick deposits may form in the profound depths of the sea, but the bottom will be inhabited by extremely few animals. Sediments formed there will preserve an incomplete record of life in the world.

A geologist's hammer has cracked open a concretion—a solid mass or globe of sedimentary rock—to reveal a fossil.

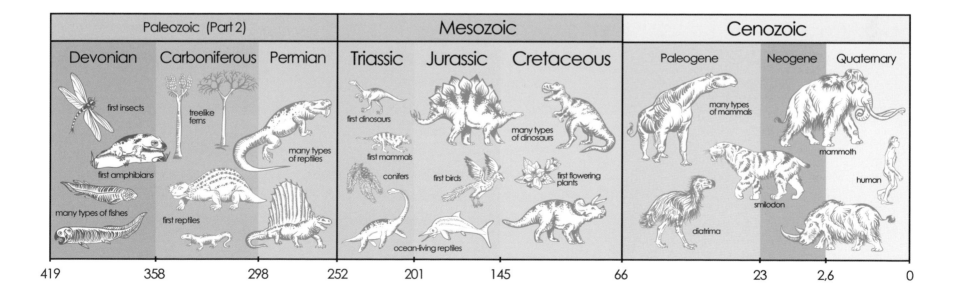

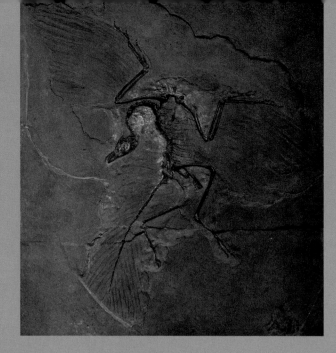

The discovery of *Archaeopteryx*, part reptile and part bird, thrilled Darwin.

Darwin's Missing Fossils—Found!

Darwin admitted that, in his time, the world's fossil collections did not show the stages that must have existed as one form of life slowly changed into another over many generations. Such transitional fossils would be a key piece of evidence for evolution—if they were ever found.

One of the world's most famous fossils came to light in 1861, two years after Darwin published *On the Origin of Species*. When Darwin heard about it, he called it "by far the greatest fossil of recent times." Preserved on a sheet of smooth rock from a quarry in

Germany were the remains of a creature with the feathered wings of a bird and the teeth, spine, and legs of a lizard. Scientists named it *Archaeopteryx*, meaning "ancient wing."

The German find was soon recognized as a transitional fossil, one that represented a stage in the slow change from one form to another. Partway between reptile and bird, *Archaeopteryx* was one of the "links" in the "long and branching chain of life" that Darwin had mentioned in the *Origin*. In a letter to a friend, he rejoiced in the discovery, saying, "This is a grand case for me."

For a long time, *Archaeopteryx*, which lived about 150 million years ago, was considered the oldest or first bird. Since that 1861 discovery, however, scientists have been able to study not only more *Archaeopteryx* fossils, but also other extinct species that bridged the gap between one group of dinosaurs and their modern descendants, the birds. *Archaeopteryx*, we now know, was just one of several kinds of birdlike dinosaurs (or dinosaurlike birds) that gave rise to today's birds.

Other gaps are filling in too. Fossil-hunting scientists in northern Canada, above the Arctic Circle, made a remarkable find in 2004. It is a fossilized fish from about 375 million years ago—a fish that resembles tetrapods, or four-legged animals, which first appeared around 363 million years ago. *Tiktaalik*, as the "fishapod" was named in one of the languages of the local Native people, has scales, fins, and gills like a fish. It also has features found in mammals but not in fish: its head could swivel on its neck, and its ribs were like those of the early tetrapods, evolved to support the animal's weight on land.

Scientists do not think that *Tiktaalik* lived on land. It probably lived in shallow water and propped itself up, or pulled itself along the bottom, with its four sturdy fins. But *Tiktaalik*, or something like it that has not yet been discovered, is a likely link between one group of ancient fishes and the four-legged land animals that descended from them.

Sediment may also build up over a shallow sea or lake bottom, if that bottom continues slowly sinking. In this case, as long as the rate of sinking and the supply of new sediment nearly balance each other, the sea will remain shallow and favorable for life. A fossil-bearing layer thick enough to resist any amount of erosion may form.

ON THE ORIGIN OF SPECIES

The Richest Fossil Beds

I am convinced that all ancient formations rich in fossils have been formed during the slow sinking of seabeds and lake bottoms. Formations rich in fossils and thick enough to resist erosion may have formed over wide spaces—but only where there was enough sediment to keep the sea shallow, and to cover the remains of plants and animals before they could decay.

During periods of sinking, the habitable area of land and shallow sea will decrease. There will be much extinction, but few new varieties or species will develop, because no new places to live are appearing. Yet it is during these very periods that our deposits richest in fossils were laid down. It is not remarkable that they do not contain transitional forms.

We have no right to expect to find in our geological formations an infinite number of the forms that, according to my theory, connected past and present species into one long and branching chain of life. We ought only to look for a few links. But I would never have suspected how poor a history of the changes in life we find in the fossil record, if not that the lack of links between species was such a challenge to my theory.

From our ignorance of the geology of other countries beyond Europe and the United States, and from the revolution in paleontology brought about by the discoveries of even the last dozen years, it seems to me to be as foolish to think we fully know the history of life throughout the world, as it would be for a naturalist to land for five minutes on some barren point in Australia and then discuss the number and range of Australian species.

Those who think the natural geological record is perfect will undoubtedly reject my theory. For my part, I look at the record as a history of the world imperfectly kept, and written in a changing language. We possess only the last volume, relating only to two or three countries. Of this volume, only here and there a short chapter has been preserved, and of each page, only here and there a few lines.

A fossil crinoid, or sea lily, emerges from the surrounding rock. Marine fossils found on land help scientists map the appearance and disappearance of ancient seas.

CHAPTER TEN

The Rise and Fall of Species

I mperfect as it is, the geological record tells us that many species have appeared and disappeared over time. Does that record fit better with the common view that species do not change, or with my view that species are modified through descent and natural selection?

We see from the fossil beds that different groups of living things have not changed at the same rate, or to the same degree. Some recent beds have the remains of only one or two extinct species, together with the first fossils of one or two more recent forms. Some old fossil beds, in contrast, have many extinct forms along with a few that still exist today. One

The mighty *Tyrannosaurus rex* is one of countless species that have "disappeared from the face of the Earth," as Darwin put it.

The workshop of Benjamin Waterhouse Hawkins, who built the Crystal Palace dinosaurs displayed in the 1850s. (Two completed models are shown on page 100.) Although an expert on anatomy guided Hawkins, scientists now know that many of the models were inaccurate. Their size, however, awed and terrified visitors.

bed near the Himalaya mountains of Asia contains the ancient remains of a crocodile species that still exists, together with many strange and lost mammals and reptiles.

When a species has disappeared from the face of the Earth, we have reason to believe that the identical form never reappears. We can clearly understand why a lost species is lost forever. The offspring of one species might adapt to fill the exact place of another species, but the two forms—the old and the new—would not be identical. Each would inherit different features along a different path of descent.

For instance, it is just possible, if our fantail pigeons were all destroyed, that pigeon fanciers, by striving during long ages, might make a new breed almost the same as our present fantail. But imagine that the fantail's parent species, the rock pigeon, was also destroyed. It is impossible that a fantail identical to the existing breed could come from any other species of pigeon than the rock pigeon. Even if a newly formed fantail looked very much like our present bird, it would inherit slight features that would make it different, because the two would have descended from different parent species.

There seems to be no reason why all the inhabitants of a country would change suddenly, or at the same time, or to an equal degree. Yet we can see why all the species in the same region do change at last, given enough time. When many of the inhabitants of a country have become modified, the principles of competition and relationships among organisms mean that a species that does not become somewhat modified will likely be exterminated. In other words, those that do not change become extinct.

Mass Extinctions

Before Darwin's time, people who studied fossils and geology thought that extinct forms of life had been "swept away," as Darwin said, by huge disasters. This theory came to be known as catastrophism. It said that the pattern of life over time was shaped by sudden, violent, large-scale catastrophes such as massive volcanic eruptions, floods, and earthquakes.

In Darwin's day, most scientists, especially British ones, had a different idea. The Earth and the life upon it had been shaped, they said, by ordinary, everyday forces that anyone could see taking place—for example, how land is steadily worn away by rain, wind, the flow of rivers, or the pounding of waves against a shore. This view is called gradualism, because it held that change in the past happened slowly or gradually. It is also called uniformitarianism—the forces that shaped the Earth in the past worked at an even, or uniform, rate that continues today.

Darwin supported the gradual view of change. Still, he had to admit that some groups of ancient life-forms seemed to disappear from the fossil record in a way that he called "wonderfully sudden." These sudden-seeming disappearances, he thought, might be due to gaps in the fossil record. Maybe "much slow extermination" took place in the gaps.

Today scientists know that both gradual forces *and* catastrophes have shaped the history of our planet. In addition to the slow changes Darwin described, life has undergone five mass extinctions. Each time, at least half of all living species became extinct quickly—although in geological time, "quickly" can mean several million years. Catastrophes probably caused, or at least contributed to, the mass extinctions.

The first one happened about 440 million years ago, when most of the Earth's life was in the sea. Huge glaciers spread, trapping the Earth's water in the form of ice, wiping out many species. The most severe mass extinction was 250 million years ago. It killed more than 90 percent of all life-forms on Earth. Scientists don't know what caused this Great Dying, as it is sometimes called. A comet or asteroid may have hit the Earth. Another possibility is a series of volcanic eruptions lasting tens of thousands of years, or longer.

A mass extinction around sixty-five million years ago—possibly triggered by an asteroid that crashed off the coast of Mexico—killed the dinosaurs. About half of all other species also died at that time, including the ammonites Darwin mentions as an example of a "sudden" extinction. Recent fossil finds, however, suggest that the ammonites and other forms of life may have dwindled away for several million years before they disappeared completely.

Are we in the middle of a sixth mass extinction today? Darwin recognized in the *Origin* that some animals had become extinct due to human actions. Many scientists now fear that activities such as logging, building, and farming, as well as worldwide climate change, are destroying species at a rate not seen since the mass extinctions of our planet's past.

An artist's vision of a huge asteroid crashing into Earth.

Extinction

We have largely given up the old notion of all the inhabitants of the Earth being swept away by catastrophe. The fossil record gives us every reason to believe that species and groups of species gradually disappear, one after another, first from one spot, then from another, and finally from the world.

Single species and whole groups of species last for very unequal periods. Some groups have endured from the earliest known dawn of life to the present day. Some disappeared before the close of the Paleozoic era. The fossil record suggests that it generally takes longer for a group of species to become extinct than it took for them to appear.

No one, I think, can have marveled more at the extinction of species than I have done. When I found in South America the tooth of a horse embedded with the remains of mastodon, megatherium, and other extinct monsters, I was filled with astonishment. The horse has run wild in South America since the Spaniards introduced it, but there were no horses in the Americas when the Spanish reached those shores. I asked myself how I could have found the fossilized tooth of an ancient horse.

But how utterly groundless was my astonishment! It was soon discovered that the tooth belonged to an extinct species of horse that had disappeared from the Americas before Europeans arrived there. If this species had been still living, but rare, no naturalist would have been surprised at its rarity. A vast number of species in all countries are rare.

A species is rare because something is unfavorable in its conditions of life. What that something is, we can hardly ever tell. The increase of every living being is constantly being held back by forces harmful to it. Those forces cause rarity, and finally extinction. Looking at the fossil record, we find fewer and fewer fossils of a species before it finally disappears completely.

Competition among species will generally be most severe between the forms that are most similar. This is why the modified and improved descendants of a

The mastodon is an extinct animal related to mammoths and distantly related to living elephants.

The megatherium is an extinct ground sloth about as large as an elephant.

species will generally exterminate the parent species—the old and new species are similar, and they compete for the same place in nature.

Instead of being exterminated, a few forms of life may last for a very long time. Perhaps they are especially well fitted to some peculiar line of life. Or they live in some remote and isolated place where they have escaped severe competition. For instance, consider the group of fishes called ganoids, which are armored in bony scales. This great group once populated the ancient seas. Today it is almost extinct, except for a few types, such as the sturgeon and the gar, that live on in our fresh waters.

The bony knobs on this Atlantic sturgeon's spine and sides identify it as one of the surviving species of ganoid fishes, which have bony, platelike scales.

Trilobites were early arthropods. Thousands of species of them lived in the world's oceans for almost three hundred million years.

Ammonites were shelled mollusks distantly related to the modern squid, cuttlefish, and octopus.

The fossil record sometimes shows what seems to be the sudden extermination of whole families or orders. The sea-dwelling **trilobites** were once numerous and widespread, but they vanished at the close of the Paleozoic era. Another sea-dwelling group, the **ammonites**, became extinct at the close of the Mesozoic era. But remember what has been said in Chapter Nine about long spans of time that passed between the fossil-bearing formations we see today. In those blank intervals there may have been much slow extermination.

The Living and the Lost

Let us now look to the relationships among extinct and living species. In my theory of natural selection, the extinction of old forms is closely connected to the production of new forms. Living species are descended from extinct ones.

The more ancient an extinct species is, the more it differs from living forms. But all extinct species can be classified either in groups that still exist, or as links between these known groups. In fact, extinct forms help to fill the wide gaps between living genera, families, and orders.

Some writers have objected to extinct species or groups of species being considered as intermediate between living species or groups. The objection is sound, if "intermediate" means exactly halfway between two living forms. But many

Researchers examine fossil-bearing sediment layers in Colorado, hoping to fill in a page of what Darwin called the "broken" geological record.

extinct species share features with more than one living species.

Some extinct groups share features with different living groups—even groups that belong to widely separated kinds of life. For instance, fish and reptiles are now separated from each other by many features. Very ancient extinct fish and reptiles, however, would be separated by fewer features. They were already separate, but fossils should show that they were closer to one another than they are today. Our best paleontologists agree that this often seems to be the case.

We possess only the last volume of the geological record, and in a very broken condition. We have no right to expect, except in very rare cases, to fill up wide intervals, and thus unite all the members of families or orders from oldest to newest.

The theory of descent with modification explains to me in a satisfactory manner the main facts about relationships among extinct forms of life, and also between extinct and living forms. And those facts are wholly unexplainable any other way.

My theory explains why fossils from layers that closely follow one another are closely related, even if they are separate species. As I attempted to show in the last chapter, we should not expect to find all the intermediate varieties between the species that lived at the beginning of each geological period and those that lived at the end. But we ought to find closely related forms in layers close to one another, and we do. We find just what we have a right to expect: evidence of slow change in the forms of species.

From Old Forms to New

Australia today is home to many types of marsupials. Studies of fossils found in Australian caves show that they are the remains of ancient creatures that were closely related to living marsupials.

The same thing is true with the armadillos of South America. Even an uneducated eye can see the likeness between gigantic pieces of fossil armor like

"We possess only the last volume of the geological record, and in a very broken condition."

The nine-banded armadillo—the only species of armadillo native to the United States—is found in North, Central, and South America. Despite its name, it can have from seven to eleven flexible bands in the middle of its armored body.

those of huge extinct armadillos, found in several places, and the smaller living species of armadillo. I was so struck with these facts that I strongly insisted, in *The Voyage of the Beagle*, on this "law of the succession of types"—on "this wonderful relationship in the same continent between the dead and the living."

What does this remarkable law mean? First, notice that the present climate and conditions of life in Australia are different from the parts of South America that lie at the same distance from the equator. Yet geology tells us that these two continents, like the rest of the world, have had many changes of climate and physical conditions over the ages.

Now consider the fact that the two continents have different kinds of animals—marsupials in Australia, sloths and armadillos in South America. Those types of life have existed within each continent for many ages, through many changes of physical conditions. Therefore, the difference in the physical conditions of life in Australia and South America today does not explain why marsupials are found in one continent and sloths and armadillos in the other.

Nor can we pretend that some unbreakable law says that marsupials should have been produced only in Australia, or sloths and armadillos only in South America. Fossils have shown that Europe in ancient times had many marsupials, and **North America** once had many more of the kinds of animals now found only in South America.

There is an explanation for how the same types of life last for long periods of time within the same areas. That explanation is the theory of descent with modification. The inhabitants of each quarter of the world will obviously leave in that quarter descendants that are closely linked, yet modified. If the inhabitants of one continent differed greatly from those of another continent, as ancient marsupials differed from ancient armadillos, their surviving descendants will also differ in similar ways.

It may be asked in ridicule whether I think the megatherium and other huge, extinct South American monsters have left behind them the much smaller sloth, armadillo, and anteater as their descendants. Not for an instant. Those huge animals have become wholly extinct. They left **no descendants**. But

Today North America has no sloths, but armadillos live in the southern part of the continent. Various sloth and other armadillo species once inhabited many parts of North America. They are now extinct.

Darwin was correct. No species alive today evolved directly from the giant sloths, anteaters, and armadillos of the Americas. But scientists now recognize the living American species of sloths, anteaters, and armadillos as members of the same order that included the extinct giants.

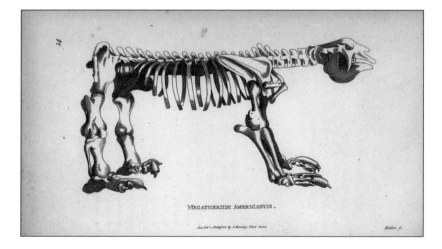

MEGATHERIUM AMERICANUM.

An 1809 drawing of a fossil megatherium. Several decades later, Darwin found megatherium fossils in South America.

the caves of Brazil contain fossils of many extinct species closer in size to the species that still live in South America. Some of these fossils may be the ancestors of the living species.

Fossils and My Theory

In Chapter Nine I tried to show the incompleteness of the geological record. Only a small portion of the globe has been geologically explored with care. Only certain classes of organisms have been well preserved as fossils. The number of individuals and species in our museums is absolutely nothing compared with the generations that must have passed away during even one layer of the Earth's rock formations, to say nothing of the enormous intervals of time between one fossil-bearing formation and the next.

A reader who rejects these views on the geological record will reject my whole theory. He may disbelieve in the enormous intervals of time that have passed. He may ask, "Where are the remains of those infinitely numerous organisms that must have existed long before **our oldest fossil beds** were deposited?"

I can answer only by saying that as far as we can see, our oceans and our rising and falling **continents have stood where they now stand** ever since those first fossil beds were laid down. But long before that period, the world may have looked wholly different. Older continents, formed of layers and formations older than any we know, may have been changed beyond recognition by volcanic heat, or may lie buried under the ocean.

All the other great leading facts in paleontology seem to me to fit the theory of descent with modification through natural selection. We have seen how new species appear in the fossil record; how the development of new forms almost always causes the extinction of old forms; and why a species that has disappeared never reappears, for the link has been broken.

We understand how all the forms of life, ancient and recent, make together one grand system, for all are connected by descent. We clearly see that the more

The oldest fossil beds known in Darwin's time were from the early Silurian period (modern scientists date the Silurian from about 444 to 416 million years ago). The strata beneath the Silurian beds were once thought to come from a time before life existed, but recent researchers have found fossils of early life that may be more than 4 billion years old.

Scientists now know that the continents have moved a great deal since early fossil beds were formed. See "Drifting Continents" in Chapter Eleven for an explanation.

ancient a form is, the more it is different from the living beings of today, and that fossils in layers next to one another are more alike than fossils from widely separated layers, because they are closer to one another in time.

If the geological record is as imperfect as I believe it to be, the main objections to the theory of natural selection are greatly weakened or disappear. All knowledge of paleontology plainly shows that old forms of life are replaced by new and modified forms, shaped by the laws of variation and preserved by natural selection.

CHAPTER ELEVEN

The Geography of Life

Turning now from the patterns of ancient life in the fossil record, let us look at the pattern of life spread over the face of the globe today. What lives where, and how does this distribution of living things fit the theory of descent with modification?

Three Great Facts

In considering the distribution of life, three great facts strike us.

The first fact is that the general similarities and differences between the plant and animal life of various regions cannot be due to climate or other physical conditions. America alone proves this is true. All authors agree that one of the most basic divisions in the distribution of life is between the New and Old Worlds. Yet the vast American continents have humid districts, arid deserts,

In Darwin's time, many people thought of Europe, Asia, and Africa as the Old World. The Americas were the New World, because they had been discovered by Europeans just a few centuries earlier.

Deserts are home to plants and animals adapted to their conditions. To other species, they are barriers to migration.

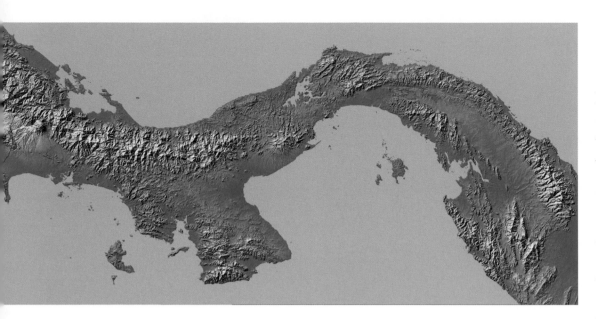

The Isthmus of Panama is part of Central America, which links North and South America. It separates the Caribbean Sea (*top*) from the Pacific Ocean (*bottom*). Twenty million years ago, there was no isthmus. Then volcanoes began erupting from the ocean floor, creating new islands in the gap between the two continents. Soil carried by currents built up around the islands until, by three million years ago, the isthmus was complete. This narrow strip of land changed the planet. It redirected ocean currents, altered weather patterns, and let plants and animals move between North and South America. This image is a satellite photograph, with land and sea shown in false colors to highlight the region's geography.

lofty mountains, grassy plains, forests, marshes, lakes, and great rivers, under almost every temperature. There is hardly a climate or condition in the Old World which is not found in the New. Yet how widely different are their living productions!

In the southern hemisphere, large tracts of land in Australia, South Africa, and western South America are extremely similar in all their conditions. It would be impossible, however, to point out three sets of plants and animals more utterly unlike one another. But if we compare the life-forms of two parts of South America that have considerably different climates, they are more closely related to each other than either is related to the life-forms of Australia or Africa in nearly the same climate.

The second great fact is that barriers of any kind, or obstacles to free migration, have much to do with differences in life-forms from region to region. We see this in the great difference of nearly all the land plants and animals between the New and Old Worlds, which are separated by oceans. The only exception is in the far north, where the land almost joins, allowing free migration to Arctic forms of life.

Physical barriers explain the great difference between the plants and animals that live at the same latitude in Australia, Africa, and South America. Their climates might be similar, but these continents, separated by wide oceans, are almost as isolated from one another as possible.

Within each continent we see the same fact. We find different forms of life on the opposite sides of lofty mountain ranges, great deserts, and sometimes even large rivers. Turning to the sea, we find the same law. No two groups of marine animals are more different—with hardly a fish, shell, or crab in common—than those of the eastern and western shores of Central America.

ON THE ORIGIN OF SPECIES

Yet only the narrow **Isthmus** of Panama separates these two groups of creatures.

The third great fact is the similarity among life-forms within each single continent or sea. A naturalist traveling from north to south within a continent, for instance, never fails to be struck by the way groups of beings are replaced by others that are closely related even though they are distinct. He hears similar notes from closely related, yet distinct kinds of birds. He sees their nests similarly built, but not quite alike, with eggs colored in nearly the same manner.

Another example of this fact is seen in the rhea, a flightless bird that lives on the plains of South America near the Strait of Magellan. Northward in Argentina and Uruguay we find another flightless bird. It is not an ostrich or an emu, the **flightless birds** found in Africa and Australia at the same distance from the equator. Instead, it is another species of rhea.

We see in these facts a deep organic bond, working through space and time over the same areas of land and water. A naturalist who does not ask what this bond is must feel little curiosity.

An isthmus is a strip of land that connects two larger landmasses.

Rheas, ostriches, and emus are similar flightless birds, but they are only distantly related. Scientists believe that they evolved separately between ninety and seventy million years ago, probably from flying ancestors.

Large, flightless birds called ratites live in the southern hemisphere. Three of them are the ostrich of Africa *(left)*, the emu of Australia *(center)*, and the rhea of South America *(right)*. Darwin saw that the various species of rhea (one of which is now called Darwin's rhea) are more closely related to one another than to the ostrich and emu, because they evolved on the same continent.

The Bond of Inheritance

The bond is inheritance. It is the only cause, as far as we know, that produces organisms that are like one another.

The differences between the life-forms of two separate regions come from two causes. The main cause is that modification through natural selection has followed a distinct path in each region. *How* different one group will be from the other depends on whether species migrated from one region into the other, and how many species did so, and how long ago.

The secondary cause of differences between the life-forms of separate regions is the physical conditions of life. Barriers such as oceans, deserts, and mountain ranges limit migration and keep populations separate.

Modification through natural selection is a slow process. Widely ranging species that have already triumphed over many competitors in their own homes will have the best chance of seizing on new places, when they spread into new countries. There they will meet new conditions, causing further modification and improvement. They will become even more victorious and produce groups of modified descendants.

But no law says that a species must change. Each species produces variations, but natural selection will act on a variation to produce change only if the variation helps the individual in its struggle for life. If many species that directly compete with one another all migrate into a new country with similar conditions of life, and are isolated there afterward, they will not change much. Neither migration nor isolation in themselves can do anything.

Modification happens only when organisms come into new relationships with other organisms or physical conditions. As we have seen in the last chapter, some life-forms have remained nearly the same from an enormously remote geological period. These species have migrated over vast spaces, yet have not become greatly modified.

What about species of the same genus that live in widely distant quarters

"No law says that a species must change."

of the world? They must originally have come from the same source, for they descended from the same ancestor. How did they become spread across the globe?

With species that have changed little since very ancient eras but now live in widely separated regions, it is not hard to believe they originally migrated from the same region. Almost any amount of migration is possible during the geographic and climate changes of long geological periods. But when the species of a genus have appeared within comparatively recent times, it is harder to explain how individuals of the same species—a species that must have come from one spot, where its ancestors were produced—now live in distant and widely separated points.

This brings us to a question much discussed by naturalists. In the case of species that live in multiple regions, was each species created at only one point on the Earth's surface, or more than one?

Undoubtedly it is often hard to see how the same species could possibly have migrated from one point to the distant, isolated points where it is now found. Still, the simple view that each species originated in a single region captivates the mind. To support that view, I will show that it is not so difficult to explain the migration of species from their single points of origin.

Many species of ginkgo trees flourished 175 million years ago, in the age of the dinosaurs. Only one species, *Ginkgo biloba*, survives today.

How Life Spreads

I can give here only the briefest summary of how species may have been dispersed, or carried from one place to another.

Climate changes must have had a powerful influence on migration. A region that was once a high road for migration may now, with a different climate, be impossible to cross.

Changes of level in land and sea must also have been important. Suppose that a narrow isthmus now separates two different sets of ocean life. If the sea were to rise and cover that isthmus, the two groups of ocean life would blend.

And where the sea now extends, land may once have connected islands or possibly even continents. Animals and plants could have spread from one to the other. No geologist will feel any difficulty, for example, in Great Britain and Europe having the same mammals. They are separated only by a narrow, shallow channel, and it is likely that **they were once connected by dry land.**

I must now say a few words on what are called accidental, or more properly occasional, means of distribution. I shall confine myself to plants.

Seeds might be carried some distance by the ocean. Until I tried a few experiments, it was not even known how long seeds could resist damage from seawater. I put seeds in seawater for varying lengths of time, then tested to see if they would germinate. To my surprise I found that out of 87 kinds, 64 germinated after 28 days in water, and a few survived 137 days.

It occurred to me that floods might wash plants or branches down rivers, and that these might dry on the shore before being washed into the sea. I dried stems and branches of ninety-four plants with ripe fruit and placed them on seawater. Most sank quickly, but some floated much longer than the same plants that had not been dried. For instance, ripe hazelnuts sank immediately, but when dried, they floated for ninety days. When planted afterward, they germinated. Out of the ninety-four dried plants, eighteen floated for more than twenty-eight days.

One atlas gives the average rate of the Atlantic currents as thirty-three miles a day. On this average, seeds might float across 924 miles of sea in 28 days. When they reached land, they would germinate if blown to a favorable spot by the wind.

Drift timber is thrown up on most islands, even in the midst of the widest oceans, and could carry seeds from place to place. I have found on examination that when stones are embedded in the roots of trees, small parcels of earth are

Darwin was right. Great Britain has been connected by dry land to the European continent at various times in geological history, most recently between about 12,000 and 8,000 years ago.

To germinate is to sprout or begin to grow.

Hedgehogs are found in both Great Britain and the European continent.

An 1861 chart shows what scientists and navigators knew about the world's ocean currents by the time Darwin published the *On the Origin of Species*.

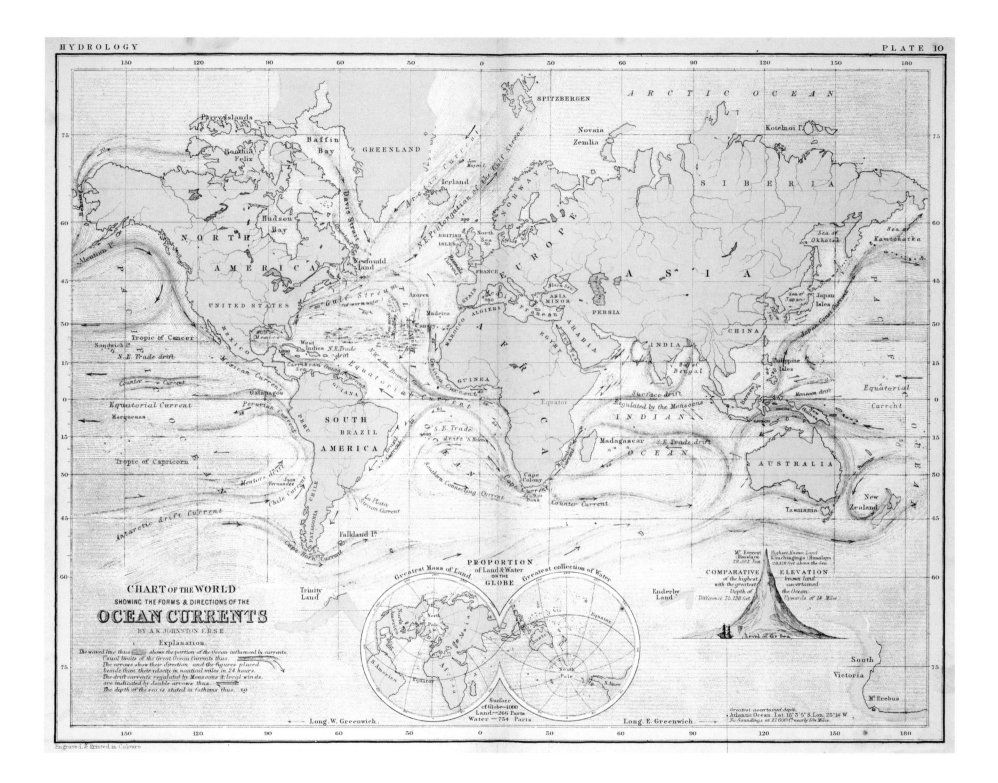

CHART OF THE WORLD
SHOWING THE FORMS & DIRECTIONS OF THE
OCEAN CURRENTS
BY A.K. JOHNSTON F.R.S.E

Explanation
The waved line thus ≈≈≈ shows the portion of the Ocean influenced by currents.
Usual limits of the Great Ocean Currents thus.
The arrows show their direction, and the figures placed
beside them their velocity in nautical miles in 24 hours.
The drift currents regulated by Monsoons & local winds,
are indicated by double arrows thus.
The depth of the sea is stated in fathoms thus. 60

PROPORTION
of Land & Water
ON THE
GLOBE

Greatest Mass of Land

Greatest collection of Water.

Surface
of Globe=1000
Land=266 Parts
Water=754 Parts

← Long. W. Greenwich.   Long. E. Greenwich. →

COMPARATIVE
of the highest
with the greatest
Depth of
Difference 75,238 feet

ELEVATION
known land
ascertained
the Ocean
Upwards of 14 Miles

M.ᵗ Everest
(Himalaya)
29,002 feet.

Highest Known Land
Kimchinginga (Himalaya)
28,178 feet above the Sea

Level of the Sea.

Greatest ascertained depth.
Atlantic Ocean. Lat 15° 3' 5" S. Lon. 25°14' W
No Soundings at 27,600 or nearly 5¼ Miles

Engraved & Printed in Colours

Driftwood can carry soil and seeds great distances.

frequently enclosed behind them. Out of one small portion of earth found in the roots of an oak tree about fifty years old, three plants germinated. A fallen tree with stones, earth, and seeds enclosed in its roots might be carried out to sea, only to wash up on a distant shore, where a few of those seeds might sprout.

Bird carcasses floating on the sea are not always eaten. Seeds of many kinds remain sound inside floating birds. Peas and vetches, for instance, are killed by even a few days in seawater. But when I took some out of a dead pigeon that I had floated on artificial saltwater for thirty days, to my surprise nearly all germinated.

Living birds, too, carry seeds. Birds are frequently blown by gales vast distances across the ocean. It is also known that hard seeds of fruit will pass unharmed through even the digestive organs of a turkey. In the course of two months, I picked up in my garden twelve kinds of seeds out of the excrement of small birds. Some of them germinated.

Freshwater fish eat seeds of many water plants, as well as seeds of land plants that fall or are washed into lakes and streams. Fish, in turn, are frequently devoured by birds, which might carry the seeds from place to place. I forced many kinds of seeds into the stomachs of dead fish, and then gave the fish to eagles, storks, and pelicans. After many hours, the birds either threw up the seeds or passed them in their excrement. Certain kinds of seeds were always killed by this process, but several remained able to germinate.

Although the beaks and feet of birds are generally quite clean, earth sometimes sticks to them. I removed twenty-two grains of dry earth from one foot of a partridge, and in this earth, there was a pebble the size of a vetch seed. In this way seeds might occasionally be carried great distances.

Reflect for a moment on the millions of quails that cross the Mediterranean Sea each year. Can we doubt that the earth sticking to their feet would sometimes include a few tiny seeds? Even icebergs, which are sometimes loaded with earth and stones, must occasionally have carried brushwood and even birds' nests from one place to another.

Drifting Continents

Four hundred years ago, mapmakers noticed that the east coast of South America and the west coast of Africa seemed to match. It was as if the two continents were pieces of a jigsaw puzzle, separated by an ocean. But not until one hundred years ago did a scientist take the idea seriously.

Alfred Wegener of Germany, a polar researcher and expert on weather, thought about that similarity in coastlines. Wegener knew that fossils of the same extinct plant and animal species had been found on both sides of the Atlantic Ocean. Rock formations on either side of the ocean also matched in many places. In 1912 he published a theory that explained those facts.

Wegener's theory was that South America and Africa had indeed been joined together at one time—along with the rest of the world's large landmasses. This single huge continent later broke up into chunks. Over many millions of years, the chunks had slowly moved into new places, becoming the continents we know today. Wegener called this theory continental drift.

After the 1960s Wegener's theory gained strength, because scientists started to see *how* continental drift could happen. The mapping of the seafloor revealed ridges of underwater volcanoes and rifts, or cracks, running through the world's oceans. These rifts separate the different plates, or pieces of

Around 250 million years ago, Earth's landmasses formed a single large supercontinent called Pangaea. By two hundred million years ago, it was splitting into northern and southern landmasses that scientists call Laurasia and Gondwana. The continents have been near their present positions for several million years.

the Earth's crust, that support the continents. The science of plate tectonics is the study of forces that move the plates around on the hot, molten magma beneath them.

Darwin realized that the Earth's surface had changed many times over its long history. Like other scientists of his day, he knew that some former islands had sunk beneath the sea. He also believed, rightly, that land bridges once linked continents with the islands close to them—such as Europe and Great Britain, for example. But he did not believe that all the continents and islands had ever been united with one another. Darwin died before the discovery of continental drift or plate tectonics.

Biologists today understand that the slow separation and drift of the continents is part of the history of life on the planet. Wegener's theory is now seen as a key part of biogeography—the study of where species live, and why they live there.

Continental drift explains why there are fossils of tropical plants in icy Antarctica. The continent that now lies at the South Pole was once close to the equator. Continental drift also explains why fossils of *Lystrosaurus*, a land reptile from 250 million years ago, are found in Antarctica, India, and Africa. When

Alfred Wegener smokes a long pipe (others hang on the wall) in his Greenland research base during the winter of 1930–1931.

Lystrosaurus roamed the Earth, all three continents were part of the same ancient landmass, which scientists call Pangaea.

The moving continents are one of many scientific discoveries unknown to Darwin when he wrote *On the Origin of Species*. Continental drift fits together well with his ideas, however—just as the puzzle pieces of South America and Africa fit well together, hundreds of millions of years ago.

Pangaea

Laurasia and Gondwana

Modern World

These means of transport, and others that remain to be discovered, have acted year after year, for the long lapse of geological time. I think it would be remarkable if many plants had *not* been widely transported.

Life in the Ice Age

One of the most striking cases of the same species living at distant points concerns plants and animals that live only on mountain summits hundreds of miles apart. Between these summits are lowlands where the mountain species could not possibly exist.

In Europe, for example, it is remarkable to see so many of the same plants living on the snowy regions of the Alps and also in the far northern regions of the continent. It is even more remarkable that the plants on the White Mountains in the United States are all the same as those of Labrador, and nearly all the same as those on the Alps and other lofty mountains of Europe. We might have thought these species were independently created at several points, had naturalists not called vivid attention to the glacial period.

Within a very recent geological period, central Europe and North America suffered under an Arctic climate. The ruins of a house burnt by fire do not tell their tale more plainly than the mountains of Scotland and Wales tell us, through their scraped sides, polished surfaces, and large boulders perched on slopes, that their valleys used to be filled with moving streams of ice.

Suppose a new glacial period were to begin. As the cold came on, Arctic temperatures would be felt farther south. Plants and animals native to the Arctic regions would move southward, expanding their ranges. Plants and animals of the once-mild regions would also move southward in search of warmth, unless they were stopped by barriers, in which case they would perish.

The mountains would become covered with snow and ice, and their inhabitants would descend to the plains. By the time the glacial period reached its coldest in Europe, the same plants and animals would cover the continent. In

The White Mountains are in New Hampshire.

Labrador is in northeastern Canada.

North America, parts of the United States that are now mild would also be covered by Arctic plants and animals.

As the warmth returned, the Arctic forms would retreat northward, closely followed by the inhabitants of milder regions. And as the snow melted from the bases of the mountains, the Arctic forms would climb higher and higher as the warmth increased. When the warmth fully returned, the Arctic species that had been living in the lowlands would be left isolated on distant mountain summits and in the Arctic regions.

This view of the world once being much colder helps explain the present distribution of the same species on isolated mountaintops. I believe that the world has recently felt a great cycle of change, in the advance and retreat of the glacial cold. When the cold retreated, certain plants and animals were left high on our mountains.

Musk oxen in northeastern Greenland. The boulders in the background were polished smooth by the passage of huge, heavy glaciers.

Islands in the Sea

A mountain is an island on land. Mountain summits surrounded by tropical lowlands are as isolated as islands in the midst of the sea. The life now found on these mountain-islands spread from place to place during the glacial period, when the lowlands were colder. But how did the plant and animal varieties scattered across the islands of the ocean reach their present homes?

Species native to oceanic islands are few in number compared with those that live in equal-size areas of continents. The barren island of Ascension in the South Atlantic, for example, had fewer than half a dozen flowering plants when Europeans first arrived there. Yet people have introduced many additional plants that now flourish on Ascension, as they have on New Zealand and every other oceanic island.

Those who think that each species was created at every point where it occurs must admit that many of the plants and animals best suited to oceanic islands were not created there, for man has stocked these islands far more fully than nature did.

Although the number of species native to oceanic islands is scanty, the share of those species that are endemic—found nowhere else in the world—is often extremely large. This might have been expected, according to my theory. Species that arrive in islands must compete there with unfamiliar species. They will be very likely to change, producing groups of modified descendants. Those descendants would become new species, unique to the islands on which they developed.

Not all species on an island must be endemic. In the Galápagos Islands, for example, nearly every land bird is unique to each island, but only two out of

The view from Green Mountain, Ascension Island. Darwin helped engineer this landscape on an island he once called "burnt" and "hideous." At his suggestion, his friend Joseph Hooker, a botanist, began importing plants to the mountain, which is now a cloud forest and national park.

Darwin's Famous Finches

In 1836, after the *Beagle* had stopped in the Galápagos Islands, Darwin thought about something the governor of the islands had told him. The island group was inhabited by large, land-dwelling tortoises, and according to the governor, the pattern of the tortoises' shells was different on each island in the group. Darwin wrote in his notebook that such variation "would undermine the stability of Species," meaning that it would show that species were not fixed forever in unchanging forms. Darwin didn't know it when he wrote those words, but among the bird specimens that he was carrying home lay even more evidence of the fact that species change.

Upon returning to England, Darwin handed over his bird specimens to John Gould, an ornithologist, or specialist in the scientific study of birds. Among them were four species of mockingbirds and thirteen species of finches from the Galápagos Islands. Darwin had not studied these birds closely. The finches, in particular, were very different from the finches he knew in England. He had not even realized that some of the Galápagos birds were finches! He thought they were wrens or blackbirds.

John Gould's drawings of four of the finches that Darwin brought from the Galápagos Islands.

When Gould told Darwin that the four species of mockingbirds were very closely related, and that the thirteen species of finches were very similar to one another but different from all other finches, Darwin was amazed. Using his notes and the memories and preserved specimens of shipmates who had helped him collect birds, he was able to determine that the different species came from different islands.

Darwin's conclusion was that all the Galápagos finches descended from a single parent species that had come from the mainland of South America. Over time this species changed into a dozen new forms as it adapted to different conditions on the various islands. One species had a short, thick beak for cracking hard seeds. Another had a narrow, curved beak for snatching insects from cacti. Clearly, it seemed to Darwin, life had been shaped into new forms by the conditions on each island and by the struggle for existence. Four months later Darwin began his first

1. Geospiza magnirostris.
2. Geospiza fortis.
3. Geospiza parvula.
4. Certhidea olivasea.

notebook on the evolution of species. He went on to write about the finches in his 1839 book on the *Beagle* voyage (although he did not discuss them in detail in the *Origin*).

The finches of the Galápagos Islands have become famous. Not only did they play a key part in forming Darwin's ideas, but they are often used as an example of how evolution works. Yet without John Gould's help, Darwin may never have discovered the secret of the Galápagos finches.

---

the eleven seabirds are endemic. It is obvious that seabirds could arrive at these islands in greater numbers, more often and more easily, than **land birds**.

I have carefully searched the oldest voyages and have not yet found a single clear case of a native land mammal (apart from domesticated animals kept by humans) on an island more than three hundred miles from either a continent or a large continental island. Many islands even closer to landmasses are equally barren of mammals.

Yet it cannot be said that small islands will not support small mammals

Many species of land birds do not fly for long distances over water, although some do.

such as rats and rabbits. Such mammals occur in many parts of the world on small islands that are close to continents. And hardly an island can be named on which our smaller mammals have not greatly multiplied once people carried them there.

Only one type of mammal, the bat, is native to almost every island, often in endemic species. Why have bats but no other mammals been produced on remote islands? On my view, this question can easily be answered. No land mammal can cross a wide space of sea, but bats can fly across. Two North American bat species, for instance, are known to visit the island of Bermuda, which is six hundred miles from the mainland.

Island Chains and Continents

In addition to distance, the depth of the sea between an island and the closest mainland determines whether the same or similar species will be found on both. The great Malay Archipelago, for example, is crossed at one point by a space of deep ocean. This space separates two widely distinct groups of mammals that live in the two parts of the archipelago.

An archipelago is a chain of islands. The Malay Archipelago is in Southeast Asia.

In contrast, only a shallow channel separates Britain from Europe, and the mammals are the same on both sides.

During changes of sea level, islands separated from the mainland by shallow channels are more likely to have been connected to the mainland by dry land than islands that are separated by deeper channels. This explains why the mammals of some islands are the same as or similar to the mammals of the nearby continent. These relationships are impossible to explain on the view that species were independently created in each place.

All these observations about the inhabitants of oceanic islands seem to me to fit with occasional, accidental means of dispersal over the long course of time. I do not deny that there are many and grave difficulties in understanding how some species on the more remote islands could have reached their present homes. Perhaps other islands once existed along the way as stopping places, but those islands have been lost to time, with not a wreck remaining.

The species of an archipelago are closely related to those of the nearest continent, yet still distinct. Within the archipelago, we sometimes see the same thing displayed on a small scale, in a most interesting way.

We see the islands of the Galápagos archipelago, for example, inhabited by closely related species. The species of each separate island are related far more closely to one another than to similar species in any other part of the world. This is just what might have been expected according to my theory. The islands are so close to one another that they must have received immigrants from the same original source. The present species of each island then descended from those immigrants. This and all the other grand facts of geographic distribution can be explained by migration, followed by modification and the multiplication of new forms.

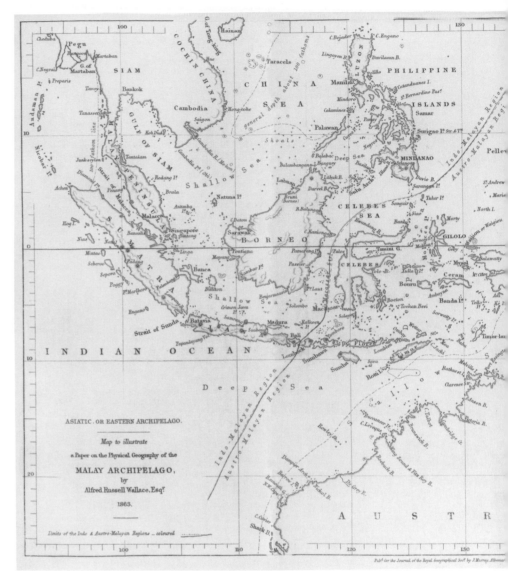

A Galápagos tortoise. Darwin was impressed by the fact that the pattern of these animals' shells varies from island to island. Unfortunately, all the tortoises taken aboard the *Beagle* were eaten and their shells thrown overboard before Darwin could study them.

On this 1863 map of the Malay Archipelago, the red line is the boundary that naturalist Alfred Russel Wallace traced between the two different animal populations of the island chain. It is known as Wallace's Line.

CHAPTER TWELVE

What Living Things Share

All organic beings resemble one another in descending degrees, meaning that they can be classified in groups within larger groups. Naturalists try to arrange the species, genera, and families in each class of living things based on what is called "the natural system." But what is meant by this system?

To some it is merely a plan for classifying life, grouping organisms that are most alike and separating those that are most unalike. It is also a way to make general statements about organisms as brief as possible. For example, one sentence can list the characters or features shared by all mammals, another sentence can list the features shared by all meat-eating mammals, a third sentence can list all features shared by the canid genus of wolves and dogs, and a final sentence can describe each kind of canid.

Male *(left)* and female mandarin ducks belong to the same species, despite the difference in appearance.

The cleverness and usefulness of this system cannot be argued. Yet there is a common belief that classification must be based on something more than mere resemblance.

Descent already plays a part in our ordinary classification. For example, even when males and females of the same species, or old and young, look and act quite different, we know that they come from the same parents, and we use the element of descent to classify them as one species.

We also use descent to classify varieties that come from the same parent species, however different they may be from their parent. Descent is the bond that is partially revealed to us by our classifications.

With my view of descent with modification from a common ancestor in mind, we can see why we are able to group all living and extinct forms together in one great system. The members of each class are connected by complex and spreading lines of relationship, forming groups nested within groups. We shall probably never completely untangle the web of relationships among organisms, but when we do not look to some unknown plan of creation, we may hope to make slow but sure progress.

What can the bodies of living beings tell us about these relationships? We will look at evidence from three areas of study: the physical forms of living things, the features of organisms as they develop before birth, and the fact that the bodies of many species contain useless parts.

Unity of Type

Members of the same class of plants or animals, whatever their habits of life, are similar in their general plan. This resemblance is often called "unity of type." Parts and organs in different species within the class are **homologous**.

Homologous parts have the same origin and structure, even if they look different and are used differently.

The whole subject of shape and structure in living things is called morphology. This is the most interesting department of natural history, and may be said to be its very soul. Consider five examples from the mammal class: the hand of a

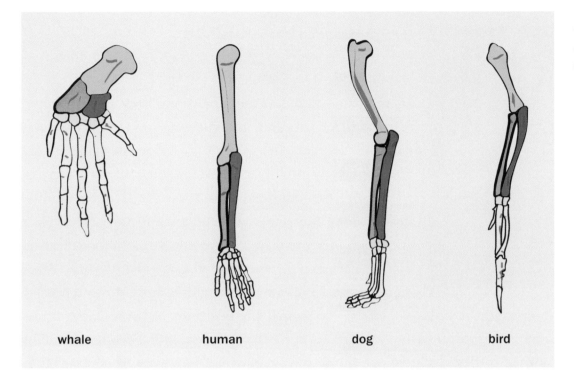

The forelimbs of these four mammals (and many others) contain the same bones, although their sizes and proportions differ.

whale　　　　human　　　　dog　　　　bird

person formed for grasping, the paw of a mole for digging, the foreleg of a horse for running, the paddle of a porpoise for swimming, and the wing of a bat for flying. They are all built on the same pattern, with the same bones arranged in the same positions relative to one another. What could be more curious than that?

In homologous organs such as those listed above, the parts may change to almost any shape or size, but they always remain connected together in the same order. We never find the bones of the arm and wrist, or the thigh and lower leg, switched. For this reason we can use the same names for homologous bones in widely different animals.

We see the same great law in the way insects' mouths are made. What can be more different than the immensely long spiral proboscis of a sphinx moth, the curious folded one of a bee, and the great jaws of a beetle?

Yet all these organs, serving different purposes, are formed by modifications

A sphinx moth *(left)* and a stag beetle *(right)*.

of the same parts: an upper lip and two sets of paired structures for handling and chewing food, the mandibles and the maxillae. The many varied flowers of plants are also formed by modifications of the same set of basic parts.

Natural selection explains these facts. Each modification along the stages of development must benefit the organism in some way, and we know that a modification to one part may often affect the growth of some other part. For these reasons there will be little or no tendency to change the original pattern—to switch the positions of parts. Limb bones might be shortened or widened to any extent, they might become gradually clothed in flesh to serve as a fin or a wing, but the framework of bones as they are connected to one another will not change.

If we suppose that the ancient **ancestor of all mammals** had limbs built on the pattern that now exists, no matter what purpose they served, we see at once why limbs throughout the whole mammal class—people, moles, horses, porpoises, bats, and more—are homologous. Natural selection will account for their variety of shapes and functions.

Based on the genetics and physical structure of thousands of species, scientists think that all living non-marsupial mammals descended from a small, tailed, tree-climbing eater of insects that evolved less than half a million years after the dinosaurs became extinct. Its fossil remains have not yet been found.

Evidence from Embryos

Signs of shared descent can be seen in embryos—animals in the early stages of development, before birth.

One curious fact is that certain organs of individual animals are exactly alike in the embryo, even when they have widely different appearances and uses in the adult animal.

Another fact is that embryos of different kinds of animals are often

144

For a century before Darwin, naturalists had been fascinated by what is now called embryology—the study of unborn life. This drawing of bird and snake eggs, embryos, and young dates from about 1801.

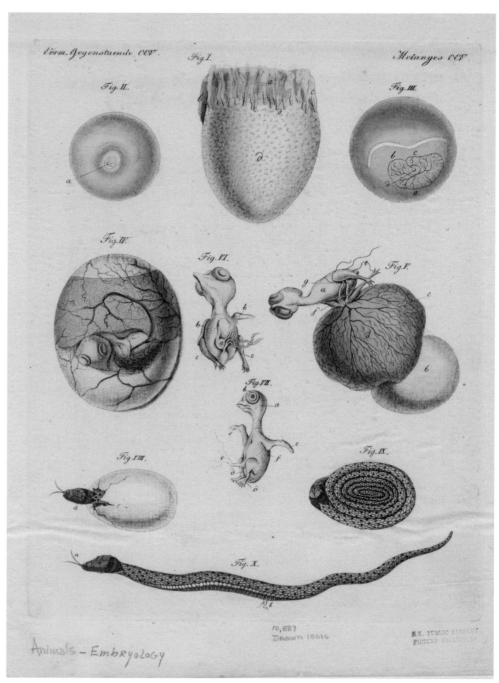

strikingly similar, especially very early in their development. A trace of this resemblance sometimes lasts even after the animal is born. Birds of related species often look alike in their first and second sets of feathers, and do not take on the distinctive markings of their species until those feathers have been replaced.

We are used to seeing differences in structure between the embryo and the adult. We are also familiar with the close similarity between embryos of widely different animals in the same class. We might think that these facts are a necessary part of growth in the individual, but why should that be the case? There is no obvious reason why a bat's wing or a porpoise's fin should not have all its parts set out as they will appear in the adult, as soon as any structure is visible in the embryo.

How, then, can we explain these facts about embryos? I believe that they can be explained by descent with modification.

We commonly assume that slight variations in individual organisms appear early in their development, but this is not always the case. Breeders of cattle, horses, and some other animals cannot tell for certain until some time after the animal has been born what its exact characteristics will ultimately be. We see this plainly in our own children. We cannot always tell whether the child will be tall or short, or what its precise features will be. I believe that **variations in individuals are caused before birth,**

Darwin's idea here fits with what modern scientists know about genetics.

but the variations may not appear until later in life. Certain hereditary diseases, for example, appear only in old age.

As all the organic beings that have ever lived on this Earth must be fitted into a single classification, the best or even the only possible arrangement is genealogical, not an arrangement based on appearance or structure. Descent of different forms from the same ancestor is, in my view, the hidden bond of connection that naturalists have been seeking.

If two groups of animals pass through the same or similar embryonic stages, we may be sure they have both descended from the same or similar parents, however different they are in structure and habits. Shared embryonic structure reveals a shared line of descent. The embryo will reveal this shared descent no matter how much the structure of the adult may have been changed and hidden. The embryonic state of each species or group of species partially shows us the structure of their ancient ancestors, before the species were modified into their present forms.

Useless Body Parts

Useless organs or body parts are extremely common throughout nature. Male mammals, for example, have rudimentary breast glands, even though they do not nurse young. Snakes are legless, but some have the remains of pelvic and leg bones within their bodies. Fetal whales have teeth, but grown whales have not a tooth in their heads. And nothing can be plainer than that wings are formed for flight, yet in many insects the wings are so shrunken that they are useless for flying. Often they lie under wing cases that cannot even open!

An organ may become rudimentary or useless for its original purpose, but remain in use for a different purpose. The swim bladder of fish, for example, is an organ with the purpose of giving fish buoyancy, or the ability to float. But in certain fish the swim bladder seems rudimentary for buoyancy, yet it has become the start of a breathing organ or lung.

After Darwin, some naturalists believed the "recapitulation theory," which said that an organism recapitulates, or repeats, its entire evolutionary history in the stages of its development as an embryo. The full theory has been dismissed, although embryos do reveal some evolutionary clues.

Rudimentary body parts exist in a limited, undeveloped, or basic form.

Darwin refers to insects that cannot fly, such as many species of ground beetles, even though adults of these species have wings. The wings no longer function because these insects have adapted to conditions in which they are not needed.

Fish breathe through gills. Darwin thought that the lungs of air-breathing creatures evolved from the swim bladders of fish. Scientists today think this is unlikely.

Myths and Misunderstandings

It was 1859 when Charles Darwin's *On the Origin of Species* introduced the world to the evolution of species by means of natural selection. Many years later, however, evolution is often misunderstood. Here are the facts about some common myths and misunderstandings:

Evolution does not change individuals. Natural selection acts on individuals, but evolution operates on the scale of whole populations over time. Change *can* happen to individual organisms. Animals may grow especially thick coats during extra-cold winters, for example, but changes like these are not passed on to offspring. They are examples of acclimatization, or individuals getting used to changed conditions, not of evolutionary adaptation. For evolution to occur, conditions would have to cause natural selection to favor animals that have an inborn ability to grow thicker coats, by allowing them to thrive and produce more offspring.

(The new science of epigenetics has shown that some changes during an organism's lifetime *can* be inherited by its offspring. These changes do not alter the parent organism's DNA sequence. Instead, they change how chromosomes affect the activity of a gene. Stress, sickness, and other factors can cause heritable epigenetic changes, but scientists do not yet know how much these changes may contribute to long-term evolution.)

Evolution does not equal progress. Mutations are random. They are equally likely to harm an organism, to help it, or to have no effect. Natural selection tends to weed out the harmful mutations and strengthen the helpful ones, but it and other evolutionary forces do not work toward some kind of goal. The history of life is not a story of progress from "lower" simple life-forms like bacteria and worms to "higher" complex ones like ponies and people. Worms are very good at being worms, just as ponies are good at being ponies.

Evolution adapts organisms to their conditions of life, whatever those conditions might be. The ancestors of whales and snakes had legs. Their descendants "lost" these complex organs when their conditions of life made them unnecessary.

A peacock with tail fanned (left), and a peacock in flight (top right).

Evolution does not lead to perfection. Darwin sometimes used the words "improved" to describe the results of natural selection and "perfect" to describe a complex product of evolution, such as the honeybee's instinctive ability to build a honeycomb of geometric cells. In reality, though, "improvement" simply means that a species slowly becomes better suited to its life in a particular environment or set of circumstances. And even honeybees get sloppy once a while and make less-than-perfect cells and combs—and the bees who make other kinds of combs are not "less perfect" than honeybees.

A trait does not have to be perfect, or ideal, to be preserved by natural selection. It only has to be good enough to give an organism a slight advantage. Even a negative variation may be preserved, if it goes along with a somewhat more positive one. Evolution is a series of trade-offs. The peacock is one example. The advantage of having a colorful fan of feathers to attract a mate must outweigh the disadvantage of a heavy, trailing tail that may catch the eye of predators and make it harder to escape them. If it didn't, we wouldn't have peacocks.

Darwin and Human Evolution

Darwin said little about the human species in *On the Origin of Species*. In the final chapter of the book, he wrote that when his theory is fully understood and accepted, "Light will be thrown on the origin of man and his history." Yet many of Darwin's readers realized that his ideas were meant to apply to all life—including human life. Some people viewed the *Origin* as an attack on their ideas or beliefs about human origins.

Humans, to Darwin, were part of the natural world, acted upon by the same natural laws and processes that shape all life. In 1871 he published *The Descent of Man*, a book about human evolution and sexual selection. The book sold so well that several new editions, including this one *(right)* from 1875, appeared within a few years.

In *The Descent of Man*, Darwin argued that humans descended from long-extinct apelike ancestors and not, as some of his readers wrongly thought, from the apes or monkeys of the modern world. Science has proven Darwin right. We now know that the ancestral species of humans (there were more than one) split off millions of years ago from the family of hominids that also gave rise to apes, our closest living relatives.

THE

DESCENT OF MAN,

AND

SELECTION IN RELATION TO SEX.

By CHARLES DARWIN, M.A., F.R.S., &c.

SECOND EDITION (ELEVENTH THOUSAND), REVISED AND AUGMENTED.

With Illustrations.

LONDON:
JOHN MURRAY, ALBEMARLE STREET.
1875.

[*The right of Translation is reserved.*]

Whales evolved from land animals that had teeth. The species called baleen whales evolved to use baleen—a comblike row of plates that filters food out of water—instead of teeth, but rudimentary teeth found in their fetuses show their ancient ancestry. The teeth are absorbed into the whales' tissues before birth.

It is an important fact that rudimentary organs, such as teeth in the upper jaws of whales, can often be detected in the embryo but disappear later in the animal's development. I believe it is also a rule that rudimentary parts or organs are larger in relation to other body parts in the embryo than in the adult. A rudimentary organ in an adult is often said to have kept its embryonic condition.

Anyone who reflects on rudimentary organs must be struck with astonishment. The same reasoning power that tells us that parts and organs are exquisitely adapted for certain purposes also tells us that undeveloped organs are imperfect and useless. In works on natural history, rudimentary organs are generally said to have been created "for the sake of symmetry," or "to complete the scheme of nature." This seems to me no explanation, merely a restatement of the fact that these organs exist.

On my view of descent with modification, the origin of rudimentary organs is simple. Any change in use or function that can be brought about by small steps is within the power of natural selection. If a change in the conditions of life makes an organ useless or harmful for one purpose, natural selection might modify it for another purpose. And once an organ is no longer used for its original purpose, natural selection on that organ will not be limited to suitability for that purpose. The organ should then be highly variable toward other purposes.

Rudimentary organs may be compared with letters that still appear in the spelling of a word but are not pronounced when the word is spoken aloud. To those who study language, such letters are clues to the origins of words. On the doctrine that every species was created exactly as it now exists, rudimentary, imperfect, or useless organs are a strange difficulty. But on the theory of descent with modification, those organs can be seen as clues to the past.

Traces of hip bones still found in whales are remnants of whales' long-extinct, land-dwelling ancestors.

One Grand System

In this chapter I have tried to show that classification, morphology, embryology, and useless body parts can all be explained under my theory of descent with modification by natural selection.

The facts considered in this chapter seem to me to proclaim plainly that the countless species, genera, and families of organic beings of this world have all descended, each within its own class or group, from the same parents. All have been modified in the course of descent. Not only the living but all the extinct beings of the world are united by complex, spreading lines of descent and relationship into one grand system.

Elliott & Fry, Photo.   Walker & Cockerell, ph. sc.

Ch. Darwin

CHAPTER THIRTEEN

This View of Life

As this whole volume is one long argument, it may be convenient to the reader to have a summary of the main facts and the conclusions I have drawn from them.

I have already presented many objections to the theory of descent with modification through natural selection, including the sterility of hybrids and the lack of transitional fossils. I have felt these difficulties far too heavily during many years to doubt their weight, but I have attempted to answer each of them.

It should be noted that we are ignorant on matters connected with important objections, such as the laws of heredity. Not only are we ignorant of these matters, but we do not know *how* ignorant we are. We do not know all the possible steps between the simplest and the most complex forms of organs such as the eye, for example. Nor do we know how imperfect the geo-

This photograph of Charles Darwin was taken in 1881, a year before the great naturalist's death.

logical record is. These are grave difficulties, but in my judgment they do not overthrow the theory of descent with modification.

Now let us turn to the other side of the argument—the case *for* my theory.

Variation and Natural Selection

We begin with variability in domestic plants and animals. Variability is governed by many complex laws, which we do not understand, yet we know that variations occur.

It is very difficult to know how much our domestic plants and animals have been modified through artificial selection. We are safe, though, in thinking that the amount of modification has been large, and that modifications can be inherited for a long time. As long as the conditions of life remain the same, a modification that has already been inherited for many generations may be inherited for an almost infinite number more. On the other hand, variability does not wholly cease. New varieties are still occasionally produced by our most anciently domesticated productions.

Man does not produce variability. But people can and do select among the variations given by nature, and build them up in any desired manner through controlled breeding. In this way man adapts animals and plants for his benefit or pleasure.

There is no obvious reason why the principles of selection under domestication should not have acted under nature. The most powerful and ever-acting means of selection is shown in the constant struggle for existence, in which favored individuals and varieties are preserved.

The struggle is constant because more individuals are born than can possibly survive. The slightest variation will determine which individual shall live and which shall die—which variety or species shall increase in number, and which shall decrease or become extinct.

Geology tells us that each land has undergone great physical changes. In the

Lionesses feed on the carcass of a Cape buffalo. The struggle for existence is "constant," wrote Darwin.

same way, we might expect that organic beings have varied under natural conditions, just as they generally have varied when domesticated. And if there is any natural variability, natural selection must come into play. If man can select variations most useful to himself, why should nature fail to select variations useful to her living products under changing conditions of life? What limit can be put to nature's power, acting during long ages, weighing the form and habits of each creature, and favoring the good while rejecting the bad? I can see no limit to this power, in slowly and beautifully adapting each form to the most complex relations of life. The theory of natural selection, even if we looked no further than this, seems to me probable.

The modified descendants of each species will increase as they become more diversified in habits and structure, because they will be able to seize on different places in nature. For this reason, natural selection will tend to preserve the most divergent offspring of any one species. This means that the slight differences between two varieties will tend over time to grow into the greater differences between two species.

All the forms of life are arranged in groups within groups. We see this arrangement everywhere around us, and it has prevailed throughout all time. This grand fact of the grouping and interconnection of all organic beings seems to me utterly unexplainable if each species were independently created.

What the Theory Explains

The theory of descent with modification by natural selection seems to me to explain many other facts.

How strange it is that a certain type of woodpecker should have been created to prey on insects on the ground rather than in trees, or that upland geese that never or rarely swim should have been created with webbed feet! But suppose instead that each species constantly tries to increase in number, with natural selection always ready to adapt the descendants of each species to any vacant place in nature. On that view, the woodpecker and goose are no longer strange. They might even have been expected.

Natural selection acts by competition. It adapts the inhabitants of each country only as far as needed to compete with those around them. We should not be surprised when the plants and animals of any place—even if the ordinary view is that they were specially created for that place—are beaten and overthrown by plants and animals that enter from another country. The original inhabitants were never adapted to compete with the newcomers.

Nor should we marvel if not all aspects of nature are absolutely perfect, or if some of them are repulsive to our ideas of what makes an organism fit for its place in the economy of nature. We need not marvel that **the sting of the bee** causes the bee's own death, or that our fir trees waste astonishing amounts of

Kiwis—small, flightless birds native to the island nation of New Zealand—are endangered because they have no defenses against non-native predators, such as cats and rats, that people have brought to the islands.

Only female honeybees (nonbreeding workers) sting, and only when threatened or attacked. The sting ruptures the bee's abdomen, releasing the scent of the bee's venom, which is an alarm signal to its hive. The value of the alarm outweighs the loss of the worker.

pollen, or that wasp larvae feed within the live bodies of caterpillars. On the theory of natural selection rather than special creation, it is a wonder that we have not seen more cases of organisms falling short of absolute perfection.

Instincts, marvelous as some are, can be explained by the theory of natural selection through a series of small but useful modifications. We can understand why nature moves in a series of steps when giving different animals of the same class their range of instincts. If we view all species of the same genus as descended from the same parent, we know that they will have inherited much in common. We can then understand how related species, in different conditions of life, follow nearly the same instincts—why the South American thrush, for instance, lines her nest with mud like our British species. If instincts have been slowly acquired through natural selection, we need not marvel that some instincts seem less than perfect, or that many instincts cause other animals to suffer, as when the wasp larva devours the caterpillar.

In the case of the geological record, if we admit that it is extremely incomplete and imperfect, its facts do support the theory of descent with modification. New species have come on the stage slowly and at different times. The extinction of species—and of whole groups of species—has been a notable part of the history of life.

Extinction, though, is almost inevitable on the principle of natural selection. Old forms will be replaced by new ones that are better adapted to the struggle for life. And once the chain of generations has been broken by extinction, no extinct species or group of species will reappear.

Fossil remains in each layer of the Earth's surface show features intermediate between those in the layers above and below. This fact is explained by their position in the chain of generations, between their ancestors and their descendants. All extinct organic beings belong to the same system as living beings, for all are the offspring of the same ancestors. All past and present organic beings form one grand natural system of groups within groups, linked by inheritance or descent

"Old forms will be replaced by new ones that are better adapted to the struggle for life."

Evolution in Action

Evolution is the change in life-forms over generations. Darwin thought this process was invisible in nature, too slow to see. But scientists since Darwin's time have collected many examples of evolution in action.

One example now poses a serious problem in health care. Certain disease-causing bacteria have evolved resistance to antibiotic medicines. Strains of drug-resistant tuberculosis, staphylococcus, and other life-threatening conditions arose through mutations in the genes of bacteria. These mutations let certain bacteria resist the effects of antibiotics that kill other bacteria. The surviving bacteria can multiply and spread the resistance trait. This case of natural selection at work can have deadly consequences for people who become sick with a resistant strain of bacteria.

Another example involves instinct in small European birds called blackcaps. They traditionally bred in the spring in central Europe, then migrated for the winter to Spain or North Africa. A few blackcaps usually wandered into Britain and Ireland during the summer before migrating. But in the 1960s, people in Britain and Ireland noticed that some blackcaps were sticking around all winter, because food was available at backyard bird feeders.

The trend continued, until by the 2000s, the blackcaps of central Europe had split into two distinct populations. Young birds of one group instinctively migrate toward Spain or North Africa. Young birds of the other group instinctively migrate toward Britain and Ireland. The two populations have not become separate species, but that may happen.

A third example involves birds that Darwin studied: the finches of the Galápagos Islands. Up to fifteen species all descended from the same parent species of South American finch. A team of biologists has been studying the finches of one small island since the 1970s. They have recorded changes in the finch population's beaks in just one generation.

A bad drought in 1977 killed most of the finches' food plants—and most of the finches. Those with thicker bills, though, could eat the tough plants that survived the drought. As a result, starting with the next generation, thicker bills were more common in the island's finch population. Then, in 1983, the island received an unusually high rainfall. Plants flourished, including many with small seeds.

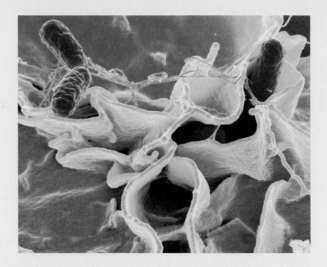

Salmonella bacteria invade human tissue cells.

Finches with small, narrow beaks, well suited to plucking those seeds, also flourished. Beginning with the next generation, small, narrow beaks became more common in the population. Changing conditions had favored first one type of beak, then the other, although both types continue to exist.

Darwin's time in the Galápagos Islands contributed much to his life's work. No doubt he would be fascinated to know that the study of evolution continues there today.

from shared ancestors. The natural system is a genealogical arrangement.

The theory of descent with a series of slow, small modifications explains many things about the physical forms of life. The human hand, the bat's wing, the porpoise's fin, and the horse's foreleg all have the same framework of bones. A giraffe and an elephant have the same number of neck bones, although the giraffe's are longer and the elephant's are thicker. These and countless other such facts explain themselves under my theory.

What the Theory Means

Why have all the most eminent living naturalists and geologists rejected the view that species have changed, and are still slowly changing? The belief that species do not change was almost unavoidable when the history of the world was thought to be short. And now that we have gained some idea of the world's age, we are too likely to think that the geological record is perfect. We think we would find fossils of transitional forms, if species had really undergone change.

But the chief reason we are unwilling to admit that species have given birth to other, different species is that we are always slow to admit any great change if we do not see the intermediate steps.

I am fully convinced of the truth of the views given in this volume. By no means, however, do I expect to convince naturalists whose minds are stocked with facts they have viewed for years from a point of view directly opposite mine.

It is so easy to hide our ignorance under such expressions as the "plan of creation," which offer no real explanation. Those who give more weight to unexplained difficulties than to the explanation of facts will reject my theory. A few naturalists of flexible mind, who have already begun to doubt that species cannot change, may be influenced by this volume—but I look with confidence to the future, to young and rising naturalists, who will be able to view both sides of the question with impartiality.

How far do I extend the theory of the modification of species? All living things have much in common, in their chemical composition, the structure of their cells, and their laws of growth and reproduction. This leads me to think that probably all the organic beings that have ever lived on this Earth have descended from some **one primordial form**, into which life was first breathed.

Researchers think that the ancestor of all life—Darwin's "primordial form"—may have emerged in the volcanically heated chemical soup of a hydrothermal vent, either underwater or in the form of bubbling hot springs such as these in Ethiopia's Danakil Depression.

Scientists today use the term "last universal common ancestor" (LUCA) for the unknown organism—some form of microscopic life such as a bacterium, which probably lived more than 4 billion years ago—from which all known life is descended.

A Revolution Ahead

We can dimly foresee a considerable revolution in natural history when the views in this volume, or similar views on the origin of species, are generally accepted.

We will no longer look at an organic being as something wholly beyond our comprehension. We will regard every production of nature as having had a history. We will see every complex structure and instinct as the sum of many changes, each useful to its possessor, nearly in the same way as we see any great mechanical invention as the sum of the labor, experience, reason, and even blunders of many workers. When we view each organic being this way, how far more interesting—I speak from experience—will the study of natural history become!

A grand and almost untrodden field of inquiry will be opened on the causes and laws of variation. Our classifications of plants and animals will come to be genealogies, and they will then truly give what may be called the plan of creation. To discover and trace the many spreading lines of descent in our natural genealogies, we will have to study the traits that have long been inherited. Species fancifully called "living fossils" will help us form a picture of the ancient forms of life.

When we are certain that all individuals of one species, and all the closely related species of most genera, have descended from a single parent and migrated from one birthplace, and when we know more about the many means of migration, we will be able to trace the past migrations of the inhabitants of the whole world, and throw more light on ancient geography.

The crust of the Earth with its embedded remains will be seen not as a well-filled museum, but as a poor collection made by chance at rare intervals of time. We will view each great fossil-bearing formation as the unusual result of the right circumstances. The blank intervals between those layers will be recognized as representing vast stretches of time.

In the distant future I see open fields for far more important research.

So-called "living fossils" are living species that have survived for long periods of geological time with few changes, such as the two known species of coelacanth, fish that were once believed to have become extinct when the dinosaurs did, about sixty-five million years ago. Another ancient species, the dawn redwood, is at least one hundred million years old. It was known only from fossils until living specimens were discovered in China in 1946.

Psychology will be based on a new foundation, that of mental powers being acquired by a series of steps. Light will be thrown on the origin of man and his history.

Leading authors seem fully satisfied with the view that each species has been independently created. To my mind it fits better with what we know of the laws of matter to think that the creation and extinction of species has been due to natural causes, like the birth and death of an individual. When I view

An "entangled bank, clothed with plants of many kinds. . . ."

all beings not as special creations, but as the descendants of some few organic forms that lived ages ago, they seem to me to become ennobled.

Judging from the past, we may safely think that not one living species will pass its unchanged likeness to a distant future. And because the majority of extinct species have left no living descendants, we may also safely think that few species now alive will have descendants of any kind in that far future. Yet we can predict that the species that will prevail and give rise to new species will be those that are common and widespread species, belonging to the larger and dominant groups.

It is interesting to contemplate an entangled bank, clothed with many plants of many kinds, with birds singing on the bushes, with various insects flitting about, and with worms crawling through the damp earth.

These elaborate forms, so different from one another and dependent on one another in such complex ways, have all been produced by laws acting around us. These laws are reproduction and inheritance, variability, the struggle for life, and natural selection, which leads to modification of forms and the extinction of some. From the war of nature, from famine and death, comes the production of new and improved forms of life.

There is grandeur in this view of life, with its powers having been originally breathed into a few forms or into one. While this planet has gone cycling on according to the fixed law of gravity, from so simple a beginning endless forms most beautiful and most wonderful have been, and are being, evolved.

❧ ACKNOWLEDGMENTS ❧

I first read *On the Origin of Species* at the age of twenty-three. Many years later the idea of adapting it for young readers came to me. I am deeply grateful to Rick Balkin, my agent, for encouraging me to turn that idea into a proposal and for helping that proposal become a book. Much gratitude is due to Emma Ledbetter and Julia McCarthy of the Atheneum Books for Young Readers editorial team for their thoughtful questions, brilliant suggestions, and multiple rereadings. Thanks also to Dr. Wenfei Tong, postdoctoral researcher in the Division of Biological Sciences and the College of Forestry at the University of Montana, and to keen-eyed copyeditor Alison Velea. All these partners in the process greatly improved this book; any imperfections that remain are my own. In addition, I was extremely fortunate to have the contributions of senior managing editor Jeannie Ng, art director Sonia Chaghatzbanian, and designer Irene Metaxatos. Teagan White's glorious jacket art and interior illustrations are much appreciated. Zachary Edmonson, my partner, was steadfastly good-humored and enthusiastic while I worked on this project. Finally, the biggest debt of gratitude goes to Charles Darwin, whose *On the Origin of Species* is not only a landmark in the history of science but a work that continues, after all these years, to engage, inform, challenge, and delight.

Most definitions here are of terms that Darwin used. A few, such as "genetics," entered the vocabulary of science after his time and are identified as modern.

adapt to change to suit new or changing conditions

adaptation the act of adapting; also, any new or changed feature or behavior that helps an organism survive

albinism a condition in which an individual's skin, hair, and eyes lack pigment, or color; the skin and hair are pale and the eyes are pinkish

arthropod the phylum of animals that lack spines but have external skeletons (such as a shell) and limbs with joints that bend; includes insects, spiders, crabs, and more

artificial selection the process by which humans intentionally produce new varieties or breeds of plants and animals, controlling the breeding of individuals so that desired features are strengthened

botanist a scientist who specializes in the study of plants

Cenozoic era a modern term for the period of geological time from about 65 million years ago to the present

character any feature of an organism that can be inherited by its offspring; a physical trait, a sequence of genes, or a type of behavior

domesticated having been tamed or cultivated by humans; grown, farmed, tended, herded or raised, and bred by humans, as opposed to existing in a wild or natural state

ecology modern term for the scientific study of the relationships of organisms with one another and with their environment

economy of nature term used in Darwin's time for the facts and forces that influence the rarity, abundance, extinction, and variation of living things; the interrelationships of all living things in a given area (in this use, similar to the modern term "ecology")

embryo an animal at an early stage of development before birth

embryology the scientific study of animal embryos

endemic found in one area or part of the world only

evolution the pattern of change in the Earth's life-forms over time; as species are modified, or changed, by natural selection and other forces, new species arise, and others become extinct; the word existed in Darwin's time, but he used the term "descent with modification" in the *Origin*, although he ended the book with the word "evolved"

fertile able to produce offspring

fertility the ability to produce offspring

fossil the stonelike relic of a once-living plant or animal, whose organic material has been replaced by minerals

genealogical having to do with genealogy, or the tracing of lines of descent

generation a link in the chain of heredity (a generation is both the offspring of the last generation and the parents of the next generation)

genetics modern term for the study of genes, which are made of DNA inside cells, and how they transmit features from parents to offspring

genome modern term for the complete set of genetic material for a species

genus (plural: genera) a group of related species

geological having to do with geology

geology the science of the materials and processes that form the Earth

heredity the passing of traits, features, or characteristics from one generation to the next

heritable able to be inherited, or passed from parents to offspring

homologous having the same origin, position, and structure, but not necessarily the same use

hybrid the offspring of a mating between two different species; matings between two species or two varieties are sometimes called "crosses"

instinct actions or behaviors that animals, including newborn or very young animals, perform without training or experience

marine having to do with the ocean

marsupial a mammal that gives birth to very early, undeveloped young, then nurses them in a pouch

megatherium a genus of extinct giant sloths that lived in South America

Mesozoic era modern term for the period of geological time between about 250 and 65 million years ago

modification Darwin's term for change over many generations; he used the phrase "descent with modification" for what is now called "evolution"

morphology the shape or structure of an organism or part of an organism, without regard for its function (how it is used)

native naturally occurring in an area, not brought by human activity from some other place

natural history the study of the natural world, including rocks and minerals, living things, and even weather, climate, and geography

natural selection the process by which favorable variations, which help an organism live and therefore reproduce, are passed on to that offspring's descendants; over time they spread through a population and modify the original form of the species; meanwhile, unfavorable variations tend to be weeded out because they do not help organisms survive, reproduce, and pass on their genetic heritage

naturalist someone who is interested in or studies natural history

niche the role that an organism plays in the ecology of a given setting, including all its interactions with other organisms

organic living, or having to do with living things

organism a living thing

ornithologist a scientist who studies birds

paleontology the scientific study of ancient and/or extinct life, usually through fossils

Paleozoic era modern term for the period of geological time between about 542 to 250 million years ago

phylum the level or category of scientific classification just below kingdom

population a group of organisms of the same species living in the same place at the same time

range the area throughout which a species occurs naturally

sediment material such as pebbles, sand, soil, and dust, created by erosion and carried by wind or water; ancient deposits of sediment, such as seabeds, are where many fossils are found

sedimentary rocks layers of sediment that have been compressed into hardness

sexual selection a type of natural selection related to mating; sexual selection produces features that help individuals attract mates, such as the tail of a male peacock, or compete for mates, such as the antlers of a male moose

speciation the appearance, development, or production of new species

species a group of organisms in which all individuals can interbreed to produce fertile offspring; Darwin defined "species" more loosely, as a category in the series from variety to genus, and argued that the barrier between species was somewhat flexible

sterile unable to produce offspring

sterility the inability to produce offspring

stock a parent, ancestor, or source of a modern species or variety

strata layers of rock that form the Earth's crust

structure the inner and outer form of a plant or animal; its appearance and the way it is put together

subspecies a group of plants or animals that share a recognizable difference from the standard or norm of their species, but are not different enough to be considered a separate species

variability the quality or feature of having differences, or variation, among individuals

variation a difference from the standard or norm of a particular species

variety a group or set of plants or animals that differ from the standard or norm of their species but are not classified as a subspecies; Darwin sometimes used "variety" to mean "subspecies," but at other times he regarded varieties as "steps on the way to subspecies"

zoology the scientific study of animals

Books

Heiligman, Deborah. *Charles and Emma: The Darwins' Leap of Faith*. New York: Henry Holt, 2009. This award-winning book for young people tells the story of how Charles Darwin's marriage and his scientific work influenced each other.

Johnson, Sylvia. *Shaking the Foundation: Charles Darwin and the Theory of Evolution*. Minneapolis, MN: Twenty-First Century Books, 2013. This overview, written for young readers, places Darwin's achievement in the context of nineteenth-century scientific thought and explores the questions, criticisms, and controversies that it has aroused to the present day.

Meyer, Carolyn. *The True Adventures of Charley Darwin*. Orlando, FL: HMH Books for Young Readers, 2009. Told in the form of a novel from Darwin's point of view, this book for young readers focuses on Darwin's early life and his voyage on the *Beagle*.

Pringle, Laurence. *Billions of Years, Amazing Changes: The Story of Evolution*. Illustrated by Steve Jenkins. Honesdale, PA: Boyds Mill Press, 2011. Written for young readers, this book tells how the idea of evolution has evolved: from before Darwin, to his revolutionary theory, and on to the discoveries of modern evolutionary scientists.

Web

Understanding Evolution

evolution.berkeley.edu/evolibrary/article/evo_01

This interactive overview of evolution, presented by the University of California at Berkeley and illustrated with many graphics, uses simple language and examples to walk the reader through the basics of evolution, with attention to ideas such as natural selection, mutation, species formation, and genetics.

Learning Evolution: Online Lessons for Students: Learning Evolution

pbs.org/wgbh/evolution/educators/lessons/index.html

These seven online lessons about evolution, drawing on resources from a variety of good websites, were prepared by PBS for classroom use. They cover subjects such as Darwin's life, the evidence for evolution, how understanding evolution helps health care and other fields, and controversies surrounding evolution.

Tour of Basic Genetics

learn.genetics.utah.edu/content/basics

The University of Utah's interactive site uses illustrations, examples, and simple language to cover the basics of topics such as heredity, genetics, and DNA—topics now part of evolutionary science, although mostly unknown to Darwin.

Every effort has been made to correctly acknowledge and contact the source and/or copyright holder of each image. Simon & Schuster apologizes for any unintentional errors or omissions, which will be corrected in future printings of this book.

The following images are from *Animals: 1419 Copyright-Free Illustrations of Mammals, Birds, Fish, Insects, Etc.* New York: Dover Publications, Inc.: 1979: pp. 2 (beetle, *left*), 11 (rose), 14 (sheep), 20 (pigeons), 24 (orchard scene), 31 (snail), 65 (zebra, *top*), 68 (wild ass), and 87 (bee engravings, *top and bottom*).

The following image is from *Early Floral Engravings: All 100 Plates from the 1612 "Florilegium"* by Emanuael Sweerts. New York: Dover Publications, Inc.: 1976: p. 99 (Mirabilis).

All background illustrations, unless otherwise indicated, are copyright © 2018 by Teagan White

p. vi: George Richmond, 1830s, public domain

p. 1: Orange-spotted fruit chafer © 2018 by Teagan White

p. 2: Freshwater and Marine Image Bank, University of Washington *(bottom)*

p. 3: MichaelMaggs/Wikimedia Commons, CC-BY-SA 3.0

p. 5: Scewing/Wikimedia Commons, public domain

pp. iv *(left)*, 6: Allie Caulfield/Wikimedia Commons, CC-SA 3.0

p. 7: Wikiklaas/Wikimedia Commons, public domain

p. 8: *Borderland* magazine, 1896, public domain

p. 9: *Hornet* magazine, 1871, public domain

pp. 12–13: Shutterstock/gillmar

p. 13: Dahlia © 2018 Teagan White

p. 15: Ragesoss/Wikimedia Commons, CC-SA 3.0

p. 16: Metropolitan Museum of Art, Rogers Fund and Edward S. Harkness Gift, 1920

p. 17: Hkandy/Wikimedia Commons, CC-SA 3.0

p. 18: iStock.com/cynoclub *(bottom)*; Shutterstock/zstock *(top)*

p. 19: iStock.com/nomis_g

p. 21: Yale Center for British Art, Paul Mellon Collection

p. 23: *Brockhaus and Efron Encyclopedic Dictionary, 1890–1907*, public domain

p. 25: Argyle/Wikimedia Commons, public domain

pp. 26–27: iStock.com/uSchools

p. 27: Brown-lipped banded snail © 2018 Teagan White

pp. iv *(right)*, 29: iStock.com/WMarissen

p. 30: iStock.com/Stanislav Beloglazov

p. 32: Keith Weller, USDA, public domain

p. 33: iStock.com/Mshake *(left)*; Naturalis Biodiversity Center/Wikimedia Commons, public domain *(right)*

pp. 34–35: iStock.com/Zwilling330

p. 35: Scots pine © 2018 Teagan White

p. 37: moodboard/Alamy Stock Photo

p. 39: Snow Leopard Trust/Snow Leopard Conservation Foundation Mongolia

p. 40: Yuliya Heikens/Dreamstime

p. 41: iStock.com/sbossert

p. 42: iStock.com/Firmafotografen

p. 43: Greg Hume/Wikimedia Commons, CC-SA 3.0 *(left)*; iStock.com/geographica *(right)*

pp. 44–45: iStock.com/Daniel Prudek

p. 45: Rock ptarmigan © 2018 Teagan White

p. 46: New York Public Library Digital Collections

p. 47: iStock.com/Henrik_L

p. 48: iStock.com/Ken Canning

p. 49: iStock.com/MiQ1969

p. 51: National Park Service photo by Phil Varela

p. 53: Ealdgyth/Wikimedia Commons, CC-SA 3.0 *(left)*; iStock.com/georgeclerk *(top)*

p. 54: Terry Allen/Alamy Stock Photo

p. 55: John Phelan/Wikimedia Commons, CCA 3.0

pp. v *(background)*, 56: Charles Darwin, *On the Origin of Species*, public domain

pp. 58–59: iStock.com/pum_eva

p. 59: Blind cave crab © 2018 Teagan White

p. 60: Olaf Oliviero Riemer/Wikimedia Commons, CC-SA 3.0

p. 61: Kenneth Catania, Vanderbilt University/Wikimedia Commons, CC-SA 3.0

p. 62: iStock.com/Jason Ondreicka

pp. v *(background)*, 63: Carol M. Highsmith Archive, Library of Congress

p. 64: iStock.com/ttsz *(left)*; iStock.com/traveler1116 *(top)*

p. 65: Frederick York, 1869, public domain *(bottom)*

p. 67: Gideon Pisanty (Gidip)/Wikimedia Commons, CCA 3.0

pp. 70–71: Wellcome Trust, CC-BY 4.0

p. 71: Eurasian red squirrel © 2018 Teagan White

p. 73: US Geological Survey, public domain